BEAR COUNTRY

The Baylor Story

Ken Starr

BEAR COUNTRY: The Baylor Story
© 2017 Kenneth W. Starr

ISBN 978-1-94429-814-2

Cover design by Kristin Arbuckle
Cover photo by Judge Ken Starr

LCCN 2016963140

Printed in the United States of America

1 2 3 4 5 6 7 8 9 10 Printing/Year 22 21 20 19 18 17

Dedication

*To the faculty, staff, and students of Baylor University
with whom I was blessed to serve.*

CONTENTS

INTRODUCTION

AN OLD STORY BOUNCES AROUND THE HALLS OF ACADEME. A PRO-
fessor welcoming new colleagues to the faculty proudly
displays a representative sampling of published volumes
from the novices' more established colleagues. The display
is intended to both impress and inspire; the newcomers
should enter their academic journey with gratitude and admiration for the trailblazers who charted their own respective courses. She then observes: "These are truly academic
books. You know about a really first-rate academic book.
Once you put it down, you can't pick it up again."

This is emphatically not an academic book. It's the
chronicle, briefly told, of a six-year journey through
academe. My story is deeply personal, but ultimately it's
more institutional than autobiographical. Ultimately, it's
a story about Christian higher education where the noble
end ever in sight is the transformation of the thousands
of students who entrust themselves (through their parents)
to the nurturing—and challenging—care of a loving but
demanding faculty.

"If not for Baylor...." So began another book, one that
included dramatic stories of students who found their
calling at Baylor, or whose sense of calling was confirmed
and deepened. That little book was a tribute to the virtually
countless alumni and friends who established—or at least
contributed to—scholarships for needy and deserving
students.

From a different angle, this little book also tells a story about Baylor, one of the premier institutions of Christian higher education in the nation and indeed the entire globe. Welcome to Baylor—and to what I came lovingly to call the Baylor Way.

1

BEGINNINGS

PERCHED HIGH ABOVE SANTA MONICA BAY, PEPPERDINE'S MEDiterranean-style campus comes gloriously into view from the winding oceanside raceway, the Pacific Coast Highway. Called to serve as dean of Pepperdine's School of Law in 2004, I was in my element. A glorious professional opportunity and personal privilege: living on campus, guiding the law school day by day while practicing law part-time with my Chicago-based law firm. As I saw it, this was a perfect combination of my professional interests and sense of calling.

I love Pepperdine. Ben Stein, the movie-star lawyer and occasional Pepperdine law prof, once wrote that he wanted to be buried at Pepperdine. Not surprising. The campus is surpassingly beautiful. The people are wonderful. No Hollywood/Malibu glitterati types. To the contrary, culturally, it's a bit of the heartland nestled in the scenic mountains of Malibu. With his Kansas charm, Andy Benton, Pepperdine's elegant president, would look out his office window in the Tex Thornton Administrative Building and observe: "Ah, another day in paradise."

And so it was. A great university with a singular location and small, manageable size. We all knew one another. And I loved my provost, Darryl Tippens, to whom I reported. An English prof by background, Darryl was both wise and learned. He never showed off, but it seemed as if he'd read everything worth reading. And what a teacher he was. Even though deans report to the provost on matters great and small, and Darryl was therefore truly my boss, I eagerly looked forward to our bimonthly meetings. We would handle the business of the day, then I would ask open-ended questions about you name it. Other than quantum mechanics and the like, Darryl was truly knowledgeable, steeped in the literature and theology of the West. One of my favorite subjects of inquiry was John Milton, a giant in the history of liberty in the English-speaking world. Darryl was, among other things, an accomplished Miltonian scholar. In the biblical sense, I sat at Darryl's feet to listen and learn.

As the years went by, Darryl knew that Andy, as president, had in mind something new for me. Our beloved chancellor, Charlie Runnels, was stepping into the retired role of chancellor emeritus. A native Texan, like many Pepperdine folk, Charlie was a lawyer-businessman who'd risen through the ranks of a large energy company, Tenneco. As he worked his way up the corporate ladder, Charlie's church connections brought him into Pepperdine's orbit, and he sacrificially changed his career course. As Charlie often said, "I like to help young people." Help them he did, with wild success.

Charlie loved everybody, and everyone loved Charlie right back. But time was taking its toll, and Charlie—a gracious but hard-working octogenarian—was scaling back. Andy had the idea, which the two of us discussed over the course of many months, that I would leave the law school and step into Charlie's large shoes as chancellor. The role would be, in effect, to carry the Pepperdine flag near and far, develop and deepen relationships with alumni, parents, and friends, and at the end of the day, raise money. As Andy succinctly put it, "Your role would be to tell the story." Simple. I was flattered.

The job had its attractions. I loved the relational part of university life, and I especially enjoyed asking alumni, parents, and friends to come alongside the university, and of course the Pepperdine Law School, to support a young but vibrant institution of Christian higher education. Asking for gifts great and small—of time, talent, and treasure—came naturally to me. After all, the overarching mission was, as Charlie put it, "to help young people," and all in the context of a rigorous, traditional Christian education. (At the law school, for example, we'd strongly emphasized the biblical call for justice. Micah 6:8, the simple prophetic call to do justice, provided the scriptural foundation for the entire enterprise of law. To that end, we launched Pepperdine's Global Justice Program, working collaboratively with established entities such as the International Justice Mission, as well as with local churches, especially Rick Warren's Saddleback Church in Orange County.)

Yet, as attractive as the chancellor's role was, I was deeply ambivalent. True, I could continue my part-time law practice, a very appealing dimension of the job. But—and this was the kicker—I would leave the law school. Period. I couldn't be both dean and chancellor. I struggled. Normally decisive, I was Hamlet-on-the-Pacific.

Then, in the autumn of 2009, a new path appeared out of the blue. On the verge of saying yes to Andy and moving on to the chancellorship, I found myself at the George Washington Law School as a participant in a conference focused on the important but arcane subject of the federal judiciary's structure. As an institution, GW was special to me. I'd graduated from that rapidly growing university way back in 1968, and by virtue of GW's terrific poli-sci faculty was helpfully guided to graduate school in political science at Brown University. My GW roots ran deep, including the rich blessing of a number of friends and former colleagues serving on the law school faculty. In short, although based in Southern California, I was back home at GW.

In a single conversation at that GW-based conference, my world changed. During a lunch break, Tom Phillips—a friend from Texas, my native state—came over where I was fiddling with a box lunch and took me aside. A brilliant, bookish, retired chief justice of the Texas Supreme Court, Tom asked me: "Have you returned the phone call from Joe Armes?"

I had no idea what or who he was talking about.

"It's about Baylor and the presidency," Tom said. I took the hint. I called the mystery man, who turned out to be a member of the Board of Regents of Baylor University. Based in Dallas, Joe Armes was a friendly, welcoming soul. He said Baylor was looking for a new president, he chaired the search committee, and he'd like to talk with me.

As the old saying goes, you could have knocked me over with a feather. I was vaguely aware, at best, that Baylor was looking for a new president. At Pepperdine, we'd been eagerly watching what was unfolding at Baylor in terms of the bold vision President Robert Sloan had articulated there. It was called Vision 2012. The underlying idea animating Vision 2012 was grand, yet readily understandable. Baylor would set out to be a comprehensive research university while remaining unapologetically Christian.

That ambitious formula represented at one level a fundamental departure for a university respected as a very student-focused, teaching-centric institution that produced ministers, teachers, missionaries, and numerous judges across the Lone Star State. My Pepperdine boss, Darryl, kept a keen eye on the ups and downs of Baylor's journey under the auspices of Vision 2012.

I knew just enough to be dangerous. That is, I knew the broad outline, the sweeping goals embodied in Vision 2012, but not the specifics, the ways and means by which President Sloan's broad vision would be achieved. Happily, my first face-to-face meeting with Joe wasn't a test of what I knew. I would have flunked if Joe had peppered me with pop quiz questions.

Over lunch at the University Club in Washington, Joe and I met on a cold, windy day the week after Thanksgiving in 2009. I was flattered. Instead of peppering me with questions, Joe—an amiable, obviously extremely bright soul—set forth what seemed to me a sales job. Maybe I missed something, and I probably did, but it appeared from his approach that Joe—as chair of the Search Committee— was trying to convince me of the attractiveness of the job.

I was honored but frankly a little perplexed. I figured a college president had to run the gauntlet of knowing the dos and don'ts of university administration. I was a law guy. Sure, I'd long had a big toe or even a foot in the academy— teaching for thirteen years at NYU Law School as an adjunct law professor, serving as a fancy-title visiting prof at George Mason Law School in Virginia, then ditto at Chapman University Law School in the beautiful city of Orange, California, not far from Saddleback Church. I loved colleges and universities. In fact, I'd served on the governing boards of both American University in Washington, D.C. and my sentimental favorite, Shenandoah University in Winchester, Virginia. All that to say, I was a babe in the university woods, but nonetheless not entirely unfamiliar with the broad issues facing American higher ed. In particular, I was quite familiar with concepts of governance, the rightful province of boards of trustees (or regents), and the proper role of university administration.

For whatever reason, my narrow, law-focused lenses didn't seem to dissuade Joe from pursuing his nascent interest in my possible candidacy. In his mind, it appeared, I was a serious candidate to become the fourteenth president of Baylor University, the oldest continuously operating institution of higher learning in the state of Texas. As I was destined to say time and again in speeches near and far, "Baylor University, older than the state of Texas itself." Texans, native and transplant alike, are justly proud of their glorious history, and Baylor was an integral part of it, as we shall see in the next chapter.

My hat was soon in the ring. I told Joe, "Let's take it to the next step."

At Pepperdine, I notified my superiors about the inquiry. Andy, the president, and Darryl, my boss, were gracious as ever; both wished me well. My possible role as chancellor at Pepperdine was put on hold.

MY BAYLOR PROJECT

I had homework to do. Joe Armes suggested I read up on Baylor, beginning with an impressive tome entitled *The Baylor Project: Taking Christian Higher Education to the Next Level*. The timing worked nicely. Pepperdine's Christmas break was approaching, and for our extended family, a Florida vacation was happily looming ahead. Every two years, we join our children and grandchildren in descending on Florida for a few days right after Christmas. The plan this year was to gather at Innisbrook, just south of Tarpon Springs on Florida's Gulf Coast, where Alice and I maintained a modest studio condo. There would also be a day trip to Disney World.

Innisbrook is a lush pine forest, complete with Spanish moss, surrounding three top-notch golf courses. For us nongolfers, however, Innisbrook held a different appeal—a beautiful family-friendly spot that our three kids adored, complete with exotic sponge diving, deep sea fishing, and tennis.

This time, however, our Innisbrook condo became my study hall. I had my nose stuck in the 350-page narrative of Baylor's bold effort under the auspices of Vision 2012. Bringing my rusty Evelyn Wood speed-reading skills to bear, within a few days I made it through the book. I then started over again for a deeper dive into this impressive collection of essays.

The chapter titles themselves were evocative, especially chapter 5: "The Struggle for Baylor's Soul." The book was, at bottom, a conversation—at times a vigorous debate—among faculty and friends who, in the end, fundamentally disagreed with one another about what direction Baylor should take.

Not surprising. At its best, a university is—as Darryl Tippens had taught me at Pepperdine—"a conversation." Everyone needed to be invited into the deliberative process and chime in. Nobody should feel relegated to the sidelines. Basic questions should be posed, beginning with

"What's our mission?" and "What does the mission mean, as a practical matter, in our daily life as teachers, mentors, and scholars?" The book expressly posed a sensitive question framed by the great debate over Vision 2012: "Can a Protestant university be a first-class research institution and preserve its soul?"

The takeaway from my Christmas reading and reflection was this: although the intentionality of Baylor's Christian mission was evident at every turn, the debate about Baylor's future course had not been resolved. To the contrary, the faculty (and alumni) remained divided about the university's basic vision. Yet through all the vigorous debate, a bedrock fact was crystal clear: everyone in the conversation adored Baylor and treasured its rich history. Just the thing to draw into the circle a history buff like me, a sixth-generation Texan who loved learning more about his native state. Rising continually from the pages of *The Baylor Project* was the abiding, passionate love for the university and its unparalleled history in the life of Texas.

I'd graduated from Sam Houston High School on the east side of San Antonio. What I quickly learned was that Sam Houston himself, president of the Republic of Texas and later our state's governor and United States senator, had moved his family from Huntsville to Baylor's birthplace in Washington County, the little village of Independence. The reason: he wanted his daughters to receive a college education. From day one, Baylor welcomed young women as students. I liked that.

Yet even with its magnificent history, Baylor was embroiled in debate and division.

Fools rush in. This would be a challenge for me, but certainly one worthy of further exploration.

My unerring guide, Joe Armes, directed my next step. En route to Pepperdine after our family time in Florida, I stopped over in Dallas to meet the chairman of Baylor's Board of Regents, Dary Stone. Joe thought we would get along famously. He was half right.

It was early January 2010. A raw, chilly day. So was the atmosphere at our lunch at the Four Seasons in Las Colinas.

I learned over lunch that Dary, a lawyer, was a real estate developer. His outfit, Cousins Properties based in Atlanta, had been the key developer of Las Colinas, which I knew pretty well because of my numerous Texas connections.

It turned out that Dary and I had shared an experience three decades earlier. We'd both been part of a lunch meeting between President Reagan's first attorney general, William French Smith, and Texas Governor Bill Clements. I was serving then as the AG's chief of staff while Dary, although young, was a hotshot in the Clements administration. I remembered this small gathering well, but my focus that day had been on the AG and making sure we accomplished what we set out to achieve with the hard-driving businessman governor. Dary recalled everything about this meeting much better than I did. I learned quickly: Dary Stone had an eagle eye for detail.

Dary broke the ice soon enough, but something seemed amiss. Dary seemed downright skeptical, if not hostile. "So why are you interested in being president?" Here was a 180-degree turn from the warmth of Joe Armes. I thought it was just Dary's style: probing, aloof, but friendly enough. I immediately found myself selling Dary. That in itself was a bit of a surprise.

I didn't do a good job of selling, but as I listened to myself spout off, it occurred to me that it was I who'd really been sold. Without making a conscious decision, I was all in for Baylor. Joe Armes's encouraging outreaches, his efficient follow-ups, and especially my study of *The Baylor Project* all combined to tell me that—as we say in the Christian life—I was being called. No inner voices or breathtaking visions. Just a slow but certain movement in a direction, crystallized (ironically) by Dary's apparent skepticism. Even with the swirling debate about Baylor's future, I found the whole enterprise increasingly attractive. I was being drawn in. By trying to sell Dary, I was in effect reassuring myself that my reading and prayerful reflection at Innisbrook had steadily guided me toward the banks of the Brazos.

There was a problem, although I didn't know it. Dary had his own candidate, a true Texan, not some D.C.-California ex-pat like me. In years to come, Dary's ambivalence, at best, to my candidacy would become unpleasantly evident. I was never his guy, and the seeds of future conflict had been planted.

For my part, I was now committed emotionally to the Baylor Project, but the leadership of Baylor's Board of Regents wasn't committed to me.

QUESTIONING

As it turned out, I was a late entrant in Baylor's presidential derby. At some juncture, perhaps at the eleventh hour, former Texas Chief Justice Tom Phillips—my fellow panelist at that GW conference back in November 2009—had actually nominated me. But whatever had happened over the many months since the firing of John Lilley as Baylor's thirteenth president, things now moved quickly. Two sets of interviews for me were arranged at Dallas/Fort Worth

International Airport, and in January 2010, I found myself commuting from LAX to DFW.

The structure of the presidential search process seemed rather odd. The search committee itself was composed entirely of regents. No faculty, no students, no alums. Where were the other stakeholders? A university is, after all, a community of faculty members who then "invite" students to come alongside them to learn and discover. At best, administrators—including college presidents—facilitate that core process and otherwise build the institution.

In Baylor's presidential search, the all-important faculty members were relegated to service in an advisory committee, a distinctly non-power group. Chief Justice Phillips was, it turned out, a member of that committee.

This regent-dominated search structure wasn't mine to question, however. After all, it had been in place for well over a year. No faculty grumblings, if there'd been any, about second-class citizenship reached my out-of-town ears.

Serving at the helm of this second-tier advisory committee was a leading figure in Texas Baptist life, Dr. Ken Hall. A pastor by background, Ken was completing a highly successful stint as CEO of Buckner International, a leading Baptist ministry that serves those who our Lord called "the least of these." Ken had taken Buckner from its regional roots in Texas to a global presence during his almost twenty years of leadership. Looking ahead to retirement from Buckner, Ken was eager to return to his beautiful home on Lake Cherokee in East Texas. But Ken also had his eye trained on another job. As I later found out, he intended to become president of Baylor. Sooner, rather than later. And he would eventually participate—in the autumn of 2013—

in an elaborate effort to move me "upstairs" to a chancellor-type role.

My DFW interviews went pleasantly enough. Faculty members probed my views on the all-important subject of tenure and the ins and outs of the tenure process, by which junior faculty members live and die. Baylor had struggled through a tumultuous period recently when President John Lilley overturned a number of tenure recommendations.

To various questions posed on that sensitive subject, I answered in effect that there should be no surprises with respect to tenure decisions. Junior faculty members should know along the way where they stood. That was the purpose of year-end reviews. Were they on track? If so, good. If not, what did they need to do to get on track? Perhaps teaching at Baylor, with its distinctive Christian mission, wasn't what they were called to do.

I also emphasized that the operative standards for granting or denying tenure should be crystal clear. Eliminate the guesswork and uncertainty. For example, what if I'm a great researcher but a so-so teacher? As I saw it, the question of tenure boiled down to clarity in standards and fairness in the process.

In my interviews, body language among the faculty suggested that I'd fielded their questions okay.

I spoke at length about Baylor's mission. I said Pepperdine looked to Baylor for leadership by example. Baylor was the pioneer—the large, comprehensive university striving to preserve its soul. Happily, Pepperdine had trained me well to think about foundational questions with respect to Christian higher education: How do we encourage students to think theologically? What are the appropriate ways, consistent with the norms of American higher education, to guide students to deepen their Christian commitment, or to embrace that commitment as their polestar in life? How do we enhance spiritual life in a secular society, with the antifaith pressures and influences in much of contemporary culture? How do we transform young lives? These were big questions, and I knew enough to be somewhat dangerous as the airport interviews unfolded.

Representing the Waco community on the advisory committee was Baylor alum (and future regent) Clifton Robinson, a highly successful insurance entrepreneur who'd recently purchased the local newspaper, the *Waco Tribune-Herald*, from the Cox newspaper chain. He'd grown tired of the *Trib's* constant drumbeat of anti-Baylor coverage and editorializing. His approach: Don't write letters to the editor; instead, buy the bloody newspaper. Brilliant.

Clifton asked me, "If you're selected as president, will it bother you that the president makes less money than the football coach?" I had the presence of mind to turn the question around and mutter: "Why, Clifton, I'm surprised the university would be so generous to the president and so parsimonious with the football coach." My answer didn't make sense, but it didn't matter. Native Texan as I am, I showed through my silly response to Clifton's whimsical query that I understood market realities. The head football coach, Art Briles, would make five- or sixfold what the president would earn. That's the way it is in Power Five conference life, and Baylor was proudly part of the Big 12, the resulting merger rising out of the old Southwest and Big Eight Conferences.

As Baylor's presidential selection process was winding down in late January, I came away with a distinct sense that I was the choice. But two steps remained.

First, Alice made a quick under-the-radar trip to Waco, where she was hosted by Kelly Armes, the delightful wife of Joe Armes, and a Baylor icon, Professor Tommye Lou Davis, who'd also served as chief of staff to Robert Sloan during the latter part of his Baylor presidency. This surreptitious look-see trip couldn't have gone better. Alice gave the Baylor Project her blessing.

Second, the university needed to do its on-site due diligence at Pepperdine. In early February, Dary and Joe visited Malibu. They poked around, asking appropriate questions while meeting with various university administrators and several of my colleagues at the law school. All the reports were apparently favorable enough.

"They love you, Judge," Dary crooned. This was a new Dary. I was immensely charmed. The cold fish at Las Colinas just weeks earlier had now been transformed into my warm and winsome best friend. Joe had put it well back in November: "Dary is very relational." Exactly so. No one is better than Dary Stone at charming the proverbial birds out of the trees.

Dary's report was very affirming of my six years as dean. I'd worked prodigiously hard to build the law school—with the inestimable benefit of a strong foundation laid by the beloved founding dean, Ron Phillips, a fellow Texan. I was immeasurably aided in that effort by Tim Perrin (now president of his alma mater, Lubbock Christian University) and by my colleague in the global justice arena, Professor Jim Gash. I also enjoyed the unfailingly encouraging support of Pepperdine's president, Andy Benton, and of my boss, Provost Darryl Tippens.

As the Malibu visit was winding down, my beloved colleague Jim Gash came into my office with an update. Dary had asked him about controversial court cases I'd handled. Jim told them about my role in a same-sex marriage case in the California Supreme Court, when I'd argued successfully that the people of California enjoyed the sovereign power to overturn that court's constitutional decision striking down the traditional definition of marriage. Jim reported Dary's response: "Oh, that's good."

Jim had gone on to tell Dary about my work on death penalty cases. Dary had responded, "That's okay."

"And then," Jim continued, "I told about your work on behalf of the California wine industry." This time Dary had replied, "Oh, that could be bad!"

Jim and I had a good laugh over that exchange. Although a native of Santa Rosa in the heart of northern California's wine country, Jim was a teetotaler. I enjoyed kidding him about our Lord's first miracle at Cana of Galilee, the only miracle performed at the request of his mother. Jesus loved a good party. So did I. So did Jim. But his drink of choice was Diet Coke.

Even with the wine stain blotting my professional record, I somehow passed muster. The call came from Dary (with him was regent Gary Elliston, a highly successful Dallas lawyer) after the February Board of Regents meeting in Houston. Dary was effusive: "Congratulations, Judge. The board has voted unanimously for you to be the next president of Baylor University."

My Baylor journey was set to begin.

LISTENING AND LEARNING

Everyone needs mentors. I certainly did (and do). Baylor alum and philanthropist Drayton McLane, Jr., now in his mid-seventies, encourages everyone at all ages to have a mentor. Drayton jokes that for a number of years, his mentors have been younger than himself, but mentors they still are.

One of my mentors was the late Steve Sample, a towering figure in the history of the University of Southern California. Steve served for almost twenty years as president of USC. As the old saw goes, he built a university that the football team could be proud of. During my Pepperdine years I looked, figuratively speaking, across the L.A. Basin at Steve's example and saw, up close at times, what a transformational leader could do with an inspiring vision and the enthusiastic support of both the governing board and the faculty. Following those two pillars of strength, alumni, parents, and friends would likely catch the vision and come on board with both moral and financial support for what the president was trying to accomplish.

Some years back, Steve wrote *The Contrarian's Guide to Leadership*. I love the book, and it became one of my principal sources of wisdom as the Malibu-to-Waco move loomed large. I needed all the help and wisdom I could get.

Steve's first step in effective leadership is what he calls "artful listening." Especially if the servant-leader is brand new (which I definitely would be at Baylor, having never run a university), he or she needs to listen, straight out of the gate. No pontificating, but deep listening. And not just listening, but listening "artfully"—with humility, open-mindedness, and discernment. So listen I did, and probe I did, beginning with the transition process.

My middle name is Winston, a name selected by my late parents to reflect their admiration for Churchill. An unconfirmed Churchill story describes a conversation in which another British leader was praised for his modesty. Churchill is said to have followed up that remark with this one: "But then he has much to be modest about."

We all have strengths and weaknesses. I have plenty of the latter. But a gift I've always had, perhaps born out of personal insecurity, is a modest view of my own abilities. In Christian terms, we call our abilities talents or gifts. We all have them, but not all of us can be everything we want to be or dream about. I was never destined, for example, to fulfill my longing to play second base for the Cleveland Indians (an odd aspiration for a kid from San Antonio, but it sprang from my Little League days, when the Indians would play an exhibition game in the Alamo City before heading northward to Cleveland after wrapping up spring training in the Cactus League).

One gift I've been blessed with from my most tender years is a genuine respect for and interest in others. I'd much rather hear someone else's opinion, reflection, or observation than the sound of my own voice. I prefer to ask questions rather than prattle on about my own views.

My Baylor-related listening began with background briefings—most importantly at Dary's home in the Park Cities, the tony part of Dallas where big shots live. Tastefully and comfortably furnished, the home was complete with a backyard basketball court where Dary proudly hosted half-court games on Saturday mornings with a virtual who's who of Baylor and Dallas athletics. Dary has a great heart, and he took a number of former pro athletes (mostly football greats of yesteryear) under his wing. This was all totally *pro bono* (lawyer talk for "without pay").

Dary was proud, justifiably so, that he'd been a Little

League coach for Detroit Lions quarterback Matt Stafford and Los Angeles Dodgers pitcher Clayton Kershaw. Dary loved sports. And he was the most avid Baylor Bears athletics fanatic on the planet.

My transition visits that late winter and spring quickly became dual purpose occasions: to attend key sporting events, especially the unfolding NCAA basketball tournaments (men's and women's), while also rubbing shoulders with key alumni and friends. I went to Houston for the Elite Eight—Baylor's men's team lost narrowly to future national champion Duke—and to San Antonio, where the women's team lost to future national champion UConn. Those trips had been delightful and inspiring, illustrated by a postgame comment by a Lady Bear starter who told the press how excited she was about going to Kenya on an upcoming summer mission trip. That was a heartwarming introduction to Baylor athletics—and to Athletic Director Ian McCaw's vision of "Victory with Integrity." While I failed to bring the basketball teams good luck, everybody was "Baylor proud" that both programs had made a deep run into the Big Dance.

One transitional trip to Dallas also revealed that an enormous amount of work needed to be done to build Baylor. The university's renowned Louise Herrington School of Nursing, celebrating its hundredth birthday, had apparently been hiding its candle under a bushel. At a centennial celebration for this institution at the iconic Anatole Hilton, Dallas Mayor Tom Leppert told the assembled crowd, "I didn't know Baylor had a nursing school. This is the best-kept secret in Dallas!"

If one thing is clear about private institutions of higher education, and in particular Christian colleges and universities, it's that the institution needs to be a well-lit city on a hill, a lamp that cannot be hid. Or, as I've been inclined to say, drawing from my Pepperdine experience overlooking the Pacific, "A university is to serve as a lighthouse." How especially true that is for a long-established nursing school with its sacred ministry of healing.

Alice promptly took on Baylor's Nursing School as one of her pet projects. With the spectacular work of a dynamic new dean, Shelley Conroy, and a beloved head of Nursing School fundraising, Janis Kovar, literally millions of dollars began flowing into the Nursing School's coffers to finance much-needed student scholarships.

Dallas, rather than Waco, had become the presidential transition headquarters. In the initial gathering at Dary's home in the Park Cities, we didn't talk football or really much about sports generally. Rather, the briefings in Dary's living room were straightforward nuts and bolts, the warp and woof of university governance. Little was said about the faculty, or even about the students.

It was, in brief, a CEO high-level orientation—the budget process, the who's who on campus and beyond, and above all, an initial dive into a long-running squabble with Baylor's historically independent alumni association which carried a pivotally important name, the Baylor Alumni Association.

Therein lay a tale, a long and unhappy one. Guiding this part of the discussion was Baylor's common-sense, down-to-earth general counsel, Charlie Beckenhauer. I learned in detail the history of what was, in effect, a long-running civil war within the Baylor family. In a daylong Park Cities overview, the BAA was mentioned more than any other key concern. I was being told, in effect, "Ken, welcome to

Baylor, a house divided." Scripture tells us what happens to such houses. They fall down. I knew instinctively that such institutional divisiveness was bad. We needed unity. I had some heavy lifting ahead to make that happen.

As it turned out, not everyone was on board the unity train.

2

ROOTS

AMERICAN PHILOSOPHER GEORGE SANTAYANA FAMOUSLY INTONED
that those who don't understand history are destined to
repeat it. The statement is wildly overbroad. Sometimes,
history deserves repeating. Oliver Wendell Holmes Jr., the
iconic Supreme Court justice from a century ago, observed
in the opening pages of his magisterial work *The Common
Law,* that in the life of the law, a page of history is worth a
volume of logic. In any event, history almost always—with
obvious and horrific exceptions such as twentieth-century
totalitarian regimes—deserves honoring.

As my transition process into the Baylor presidency
drew to a close, and our Malibu-to-Waco journey via I-10,
I-20, and I-35 loomed ahead, I increasingly steeped myself
in the rich history of the university I'd already come to
love. Baylor's story is one I never tired of repeating, year
after year, even to folks who knew a lot of that history. Like
alluvial soil, my knowledge slowly but surely broadened and
deepened. The history of Baylor University was glorious. I
was proud—and deeply thankful—to be stepping into that
unfolding story.

INSPIRED LEADERS
Briefly told, Baylor University's founding was the
culmination of inspired leadership. Two Baptist pastors,

James Huckins of Georgia and William Tryon of New York, were present at the creation. They'd "GTT"—gone to Texas—as Baptist missionaries in the early days of the Texas Republic (1836–1845). A third key leader was Robert Emmett Bledsoe Baylor, a Kentucky-born lawyer, politician, and veteran of the War of 1812. Baylor came from good stock; his ancestor, Robert de Balliol, was founder of the ancient college at Oxford that bears his good name.

Born to God-fearing folk, Robert E. B. Baylor was a contrarian. He was openly agnostic until a road-to-Damascus conversion experience in Alabama. Thereafter, this former Kentucky state representative and U.S. congressman from Alabama (his first adopted state) displayed the zeal of the newly converted. He became a lay preacher who then took on the noble mission of GTT. In the Texas Republic, Baylor quickly became a leader—both as a judge on the Texas Supreme Court (again, during the republic days) and as a powerful pulpit presence. It's said that Judge Baylor, who rode horseback to carry out his far-flung judicial duties, held court by day and preached by night.

These three core members of the Baptist leadership team drew up plans for a university that would be, in their soaring words, "capable of enlargement and development to meet the needs of all ages to come." The university, which came close to being named for William Tryon, would be coeducational from the get-go. And so the Baylor story began in the small village of Independence in the gently rolling hills of beautiful Washington County, not far from the makeshift capital, Washington-on-the-Brazos, where Texas independence was declared in March 1836.

For his part, Judge Baylor delivered law lectures to the

undergrads, since no law school existed in Texas in the days of the republic.

Through thick and thin, the university survived. By God's grace and the hard work of generations, it grew and prospered, although the curtain nearly came down on the twenty-year-old institution in the wake of the Civil War. President William Carey Crane, whose name lives on in the form of Baylor's renowned Crane Scholars program, raised money (and contributed his own) to prevent the university's property from being sold at a sheriff's auction on the courthouse steps in Brenham, the county seat.

Baylor University endured.

A WESTWARD MOVE

For much of our history, Americans have looked westward. Horace Greeley famously urged his generation, "Go west, young man"; Baylor University itself was part and parcel of that historic westward movement. When Americans uprooted themselves and followed the sun toward westerly destinations, they took with them an abiding faith in education. Not just the three Rs. American pioneers were committed first and foremost to building a better life for themselves, but more broadly to serving as keepers and transmitters of a proud civilization.

Colleges and universities as well as one-room schoolhouses were integral parts of the American spirit. Consider that at the tragic outbreak of the Civil War, there were more colleges and universities in Ohio than in the length and breadth of Great Britain. That astounding statistic makes the broader point: Americans believed, much more so than their British cousins, in higher education, and not just for the cultural elite. This moral commitment to human flourishing—and to the spirit of human liberty—was baked into Americans' democratic and egalitarian outlook on life.

Overwhelmingly, those fledgling colleges and universities established during the course of America's westward movement were explicitly tethered to a Christian denomination or tradition. That, of course, was destined to change. But not at Baylor.

So it was that Baylor—now forty years old—packed up and moved westward. Specifically, opportunity beckoned to the northwest, a hundred miles from Independence, along the banks of the Brazos River. The Texas Baptist leadership was responding wisely to the circumstances developing around them. Time—and the railroad—were passing the village of Independence by. In opportune fashion, Waco, founded four years after Baylor's creation, put out a "Y'all come" welcome sign.

It worked. A generation after Baylor had opened its doors in southeast Texas, the university in 1886 combined forces with Waco University, a struggling Baptist-affiliated institution. The institutional merger proved successful, as did the move upriver, launching Baylor's second chapter in what now became its permanent home. None of the three founders, alas, lived to see it.

The farsighted visionary behind this westward move was Rufus Burleson, who served two different stints as university president. Burleson was prodigiously energetic, both as a leader in Christian higher education and as a pulpit pastor. Famously, Burleson had baptized Sam Houston, whose initials remain carved indelibly in the fourth pew of the oldest Baptist Church in the state—back in Independence, where Burleson served as pastor as well as university president. "All your sins are now washed away," assured Pastor Burleson. General Houston's response: "I feel sorry for the fish downstream." The proud but humbled president of Texas—and later, during statehood, its governor and senator—had lived a robustly colorful life.

Burleson laid the foundation at Baylor for what later became a period of extraordinary institutional growth. His great contribution was to preserve the institution, especially during economic hard times.

Burleson's imposing statue enduringly graces the campus quadrangle that bears his name. Sidewalks crisscross Burleson Quad, teeming with students headed to and from classes. The quad is a popular gathering place, leading up to Old Main, filled with the rich history of Baylor's academic life.

Among the early students at Baylor's new site in Waco was a transformational future leader, Samuel Palmer Brooks. The youthful Brooks would go on to lead Baylor to heights not even the founding generation could have imagined.

THREE BAYLORS

In the university's rich history, there have, in effect, been three Baylors—one for each of the three centuries its institutional life has spanned. The nineteenth century witnessed Baylor's founding, followed forty years later by the move to Waco. The institution thereby positioned itself to become twentieth-century Baylor—shaped especially in that century's first three decades under the leadership of Samuel Palmer Brooks, a graduate of both Baylor and Yale. Later came the throes and challenges of the Great

Depression, two World Wars, cultural and racial crises erupting in the sixties, and hard-fought theological battles within Baptist life; through it all, Baylor blossomed and grew. That growth laid the foundation in turn for twenty-first-century Baylor, captured and conveyed by Vision 2012 and *Pro Futuris*.

In a moral and figurative sense, Baylor in the twentieth century had become Baylor-Brooks University. Summoned from Yale to the Baylor presidency, the youthful but extraordinarily talented Samuel Palmer Brooks embarked on a stunningly audacious pro-growth campaign. When he decamped from his Yale sojourn under New England's elms and rediscovered the magnificent live oak trees of central Texas, Brooks dreamed dreams.

In our own time, Baylor's generous alum and donor Drayton McLane Jr., advises: "Dream big. It's free." Like the biblical Joseph of old, Brooks was a dreamer if not an interpreter of dreams. But he didn't just dream. Samuel Palmer Brooks executed. Brilliantly so.

During his almost three-decade tenure as president, he oversaw no less than the tenfold expansion of Baylor's student body, from only three hundred to more than three thousand young men and women.

To build a sense of continuing community, Brooks launched Baylor's now-storied homecoming—the oldest collegiate homecoming celebration in the nation. Baylor athletics flourished.

Above all, Brooks peered into the future and saw the urgent need for universities to engage in medical and health care education and training. But not medical education standing alone. Out of the fertile imagination of Samuel Palmer Brooks emerged the world-renowned

Baylor College of Medicine, founded in Dallas and now situated in Houston, and its companion institution, which is now the Louise Herrington School of Nursing. The Baylor School of Dentistry (now part of the Texas A&M system) and the Baylor School of Pharmacy rounded out this comprehensive master plan for medical education.

The expansive Brooksian vision also contemplated the practical application of these healing ministries, and thus was born the Baylor University Medical Center in Dallas, now the home of the enormous and rapidly growing Baylor Scott & White health care system. Consider the doubleheader brilliance of Brooks's bold strokes: Baylor inserted itself on the higher-education ground floor by expanding into medicine and health; equally wisely, it chose as the center for this bold expansion the dynamic future metroplex of Dallas-Fort Worth. Brooks's fertile imagination saw soon-to-explode Big D as the place for Baylor's expansion.

And so, to this day, although the institutions are independent, the Baylor banner proudly adorns world-renowned medical institutions in both Dallas and Houston in the vitally important arenas of education and health care. What Baylor Scott & White aptly dubs "the Christian ministry of healing" lies at the heart of what Judge Baylor's surname connotes not only in Texas, but around the world.

ADDING THE MISSING ELEMENT

But something was missing. The founders' vision—augmented a half century later by the launch of Samuel Palmer Brooks's expansive, pro-growth policies—oddly omitted an integral component of what is traditionally included under the umbrella of university life: the strong emphasis on postgraduate education and research.

From the get-go, the founders had embraced the broader, bolder descriptor of "University" rather than the more limited moniker of "College." It was, after all, "Baylor University" that opened its doors in the mid-nineteenth century, not "Baylor College," which would have been a humbler choice, intentionally and exclusively focused on the undergraduate experience.

The ancients' practical wisdom included the simple admonition, "Know thyself." Institutions as well as individuals need to know themselves. This brings into sharp relief the pivotal element of institutional mission: Who are we? What are we seeking to achieve? Like an eternal flame, these are enduring issues, evergreen questions always worthy of exploration and discussion.

Baylor's mission, emphasizing the preparation of students for "worldwide leadership and service," seems explicitly directed toward the historic undergraduate experience characteristic of colleges, as opposed to the mission and goal of research universities. But the Baylor mission was sufficiently elastic that this missing element of university life was added in the mid-twentieth century. The addition was the inspired brainchild of Dr. J. L. Armstrong, chair of the English Department and a grassroots visionary and leading voice among the steadily growing Baylor faculty.

Many transformational ideas in university life emanate from the faculty, then bubble up ultimately to senior administrators and governing boards for review and approval. In academic life, top-down directives regarding academic purpose and mission tend not to work; they frequently create tensions, resistance, and outright opposition. In contrast, grassroots innovations tend naturally to carry with them the moral force flowing from their origins at the institutional core—among faculty, who of course stand shoulder to shoulder not only with one another but with students, who are the unifying reason for university life in the first place. Faculty and students together comprise the key. The rest of us—administrators and staff members—are just hired help, or in the case of governing boards, volunteers called to support the enterprise by time, talents, and treasure.

With his great wisdom and vast learning, Dr. Armstrong knew the time had come for Baylor to launch what would become a full-fledged graduate school—going beyond Baylor's well-established schools for professional training in medicine and law. Dr. Armstrong was not only a magnificent teacher and mentor; he dreamed great dreams in the spirit of both Judge Baylor and Samuel Palmer Brooks. Dr. Armstrong's vision was to see Baylor University become not only a seat of education, but also a trainer of future scholars and researchers to enter and explore the proverbial frontiers of knowledge. In 1951, Baylor's PhD in English was the first of what are now over thirty doctoral programs enriching Baylor's intellectual life. Twentieth-century Baylor had now become, so to speak, Baylor-Brooks-Armstrong University.

In a way, the choice of disciplines to launch this new era was rather odd. After all, for half a century, Baylor had been a leading national light in medical education. A doctoral program in chemistry or biology would have seemed a more natural fit. The unexpected turn toward the humanities came for one simple reason: energetic and determined leadership. By God's grace and the pluck of folks like Dr. Armstrong, the development of a research university began with baby steps undertaken by those blessed with the gifts to make good things happen, and who stepped up and courageously chose to lead.

In short, twentieth-century Baylor became a place for serious scholars, not simply talented, caring teachers who mentor their students and encourage them to be all that God means for them to be on their life's journey. But with this broadened sense of institutional self-definition, one overarching constant remained: the focus on great teaching and mentoring. This was not to be compromised. Graduate research, doctoral dissertations, and other elements of high academic striving were not to serve as the substitute or replacement for a mission-centric concern with the transformational undergraduate experience.

Even with the steady growth of doctoral programs over the last half of the twentieth century, Baylor in heart and soul was to remain, as it were, Baylor College. Therein lay the seeds of tension for what would become, early in the twenty-first century, a source of friction and division. The Baylor faculty—and many alumni—would become a house divided. That division would lead to the removal of President Robert Sloan, the first of three presidents to be fired over the span of a single decade.

LIVING STRUCTURES

College and university campuses are no exception to the general rule that buildings, by their nature, make statements. The buildings gracing a campus are living statements and imposing embodiments of human hopes and dreams.

So it was that twenty-first-century Baylor was ushered in by a building frenzy, echoing the hope-filled dreams of Samuel Palmer Brooks almost exactly a century earlier. Four buildings—and a stadium—illustrate the point.

First, the Baylor Science Building. Its predecessor, the iconic Mars McLean Science Building, had welcomed thousands of science (especially pre-med) students into its nooks and crannies, serving the university well for many decades. But science marches on, whereas Mars McLean remained unchanged and showed its age. Jokes emerged from the increasingly dank labs: "My high school chemistry lab was better equipped than this." Not good, especially for a university whose name was inextricably linked to medical education and care.

No donor had come forth to meet this increasingly exigent need, but Baylor's early twenty-first-century leadership determined that to serve its students—and ultimately the Christian ministry of healing—Mars McLean should be replaced.

Constructing that replacement began with a leap of faith. Instead of waiting for philanthropy to open the doors to progress, the university leadership went to the marketplace. Baylor went voluntarily into debt. This represented a sea change in Baylor policy. Prudent management principles had long guided Baylor leaders to eschew debt. Raise the money, then build the building—this embodied the long-ascendant approach to capital projects, and it had served the university well.

The new Baylor Science Building thus embodied a new manifestation of the spirit of can-do optimism deeply embedded in Baylor's institutional DNA. It manifested, boldly, the ethos that I came to call the Baylor Way.

Similarly, the Baylor Research and Innovation Collaborative (BRIC) reflected those enduring values, plus something elusive in ordinary human experience: soaring creativity. Some folks—especially real estate developers—

have the enviable gift to cast an eye on a vacant piece of land and imagine a vibrant, pulsing enterprise, a glittering new home, or whatever the developer discerns as a better use for raw land than growing weeds or grazing cattle. Ditto for a worn-out building serving little purpose.

During World War II, General Tire had opened a huge manufacturing plant on the outskirts of Waco. After General Tire shuttered the plant, it stood empty for decades. Then imagination and creativity brought new life there. A classic private-public partnership was formed by virtue of the generosity of future regent Clifton Robinson and Bland Cromwell, a leading Waco real estate broker and investor. BRIC was the result.

This 330,000-square-foot facility proudly hosts the research activity of Baylor's growing engineering enterprise, the path-breaking laboratories of renowned physicist Marlan Scully (who occupies chairs at both Princeton and Texas A&M), as well as private, for-profit enterprises. Scientists and engineers from around the world now call BRIC their professional home, as skilled knowledge-workers carry out projects that deepen human understanding and, in highly practical ways, promote human flourishing. In the process, as BRIC fills out its expansive reach, the makings of a broader research park are increasingly evident.

A third example of twenty-first-century Baylor is the Paul F. Foster Campus for Business and Innovation. This gleaming new facility—made possible by a gift from Baylor alum Paul F. Foster, an extraordinary business leader in his adopted city of El Paso—embodies the dream of Terry Maness, the beloved dean of Baylor's Hankamer School of Business. Like much of contemporary education, learning at the Foster Campus is experiential and cooperative. The old days of learned professors droning on in lecture style, with dutiful students hanging on every wise word and carefully penning copious notes, had passed into history. Resulting from years of calls on alumni and friends, Foster Campus's state-of-the-art facility powerfully lends itself to shared learning.

Symbolically, directly across Bagby Street from the Foster Campus is East Village, a living and learning center hosting engineering and pre-med students. Strategically situated between Foster Campus and East Village is the warmly inviting Elliston Chapel, a new sacred place serving as a physical reminder of Baylor's spiritual roots and unapologetic Christian culture. (Gary Elliston, who'd been present with Dary Stone for the February 2010 phone call informing me that I'd become Baylor's fourteenth president, generously financed this new jewel.)

Finally, and fittingly for high-stakes college athletics, on the north bank of the Brazos rises McLane Stadium, an extraordinary facility that hosts hundreds of events each year. Football may be king, but McLane Stadium is a beehive of activity, a go-to gathering place for business deal-making or simply enjoying the fellowship of the lunch or dinner table.

Most dramatically, no longer were Saturday football games played two miles off campus, an odd Baylor tradition dating back to the early 1950s with the opening of Floyd Casey Stadium. To be sure, football greats and future NFL standouts had displayed their skills at the old stadium, which in its closing days witnessed the exploits of 2011 Heisman Trophy winner Robert Griffin III. But Floyd Casey Stadium reflected twentieth-century Baylor—solid, dependable, but lacking in imagination and excitement. McLane Stadium changed all that, embodying once again a collaboration with the Waco community. As had academics and research, Baylor athletics had entered the twenty-first century.

Judge Baylor, along with Pastors Tryon and Huckins, plus Samuel Palmer Brooks and those who followed in their servant-leadership footsteps over the span of a century and a half, would have been very proud indeed.

3

ROOKIE

THE BIG 12 CONFERENCE BRIEFING BOOK LANDED ON MY DESK AT Pepperdine just a few days before my launch eastward to Texas from the Santa Monica Mountains. A brief message from Ian McCaw, Baylor's Canadian-born athletic director, suggested the first major order of business awaiting me on June 1, 2010 was the annual gathering of the Big 12 presidents, chancellors, athletic directors and the like. From all appearances, I expected an entirely routine gathering at the Intercontinental Hotel in Kansas City.

The issues emerging out of the book's limited contents seemed a bit arcane, and certainly no hot potatoes were evident. The nomenclature, though, was frustratingly unfamiliar. "Faculty Athletic Representative" was, for example, an alien concept. It shouldn't have been, but my quick thumb-through of the briefing materials suggested that I was quite the ignoramus in this brave new world of intercollegiate athletics. I knew something about law and law schools, but the world of big-time college sports was virtually terra incognita. I liked sports well enough, but when it came to the business of athletics, I was wet behind the ears.

That changed overnight. Barely had I learned the entry code to the president's office in Pat Neff Hall than I was off to up-to-date Kansas City for what turned out to be a historic, fractious meeting. Appearances, as with the proverbial calm before the storm, had been entirely deceptive. Unbeknownst to this greenhorn, the Big 12 Conference had been experiencing stress and strain. Above all, an Orwellian *Animal Farm*-like philosophy was the ruling order of the day. That is, the twelve conference members were not in fact equal. Some, such as the Longhorns of Texas and the Sooners of Oklahoma, were more equal than others—especially with respect to the all-important issue of revenue sharing.

That bedrock reality created a huge fault line, largely hidden from public view. Equally ominous was the sparkling new Longhorn Network, a one-institution network built for the state's flagship university in Austin by the colossus of the contemporary sports world, ESPN. What would the Longhorn Network mean for the rest of the conference? There was nothing like it anywhere.

Skepticism abounded. Fears ran rampant. The boiling point was reached when news came that the Longhorn Network might well be televising high school football games. That nice touch would likely constitute, in college athletics jargon, an "unfair competitive advantage." Think of the recruiting potential with tomorrow's collegiate superstars strutting under Friday night lights on the nationwide Longhorn Network. Why not trade that La Vega Pirates or Waco High Lions uniform for a burnt orange jersey in Austin, and continue displaying your future NFL talents on national television?

The fear, which was deep-rooted, was this: The one "have" institution in the conference would ride away with one conference championship after another, leaving the eleven have-nots languishing in the dust. None of this, needless to say, was in the arcana-filled briefing book. I went in blind.

The Big 12 was the newest of the Power Five conferences. As such, the conference lacked great traditions that marked the Big Ten or the SEC. It was a cobbled-together assembly of schools. The partial remnant of the old Southwest Conference had limped northward out of the rubble and teamed up with the cohesive but miniaturized Big Eight, led by two football giants, the Oklahoma Sooners and the Nebraska Cornhuskers. (Early on, I learned that the N on Cornhusker football helmets stands for knowledge. But I digress.)

All this, and more, awaited the greenhorn from Baylor, who just two days earlier was a law school dean in Malibu. But first, a courtesy call was in order. Baylor has nineteen intercollegiate athletic programs, and Baylor Nation is justly proud of each and every one. National championships were elusive throughout the twentieth century, but the twenty-first century ushered in a new era with national laurel wreaths in men's tennis in 2004 and women's basketball in 2005. (In more recent years, Baylor's new program in acrobatics and tumbling won back-to-back national championships under the guiding hand of Coach Felissa Mulkey, no relation to Kim Mulkey, the extraordinary Lady Bears basketball coach.)

To be sure, Olympic gold medals were part and parcel of Baylor's fabled track and field program. And football had its glory moments, with legendary Coach Grant Teaff leading the Bears to Southwest Conference championships against all odds—including the magical "Miracle on the Brazos," a dramatic, come-from-behind upset victory over the Longhorns in 1974. But with the exceptions of men's tennis, and the Kim Mulkey-led Lady Bears, national championships had been elusive.

In American collegiate sports, football is king (barring exceptions such as basketball at Kansas or Kentucky). Football revenue subsidizes everything else (except for men's basketball, which is usually revenue-positive). It was thus appropriate for me, before heading to the Show-Me State for the conference meeting, to stop by and say hello to our up-and-coming head football coach, Art Briles, who was already the most popular figure on Baylor's campus. After greeting him, I asked a simple question: "What do you need?" I knew he was handsomely compensated, so I wasn't concerned about his making a pitch for a salary hike, especially in a courtesy meeting such as this one. Coach was charming, but crystal clear: "We need an on-campus stadium." He added, "That's a need, not a want."

That was the first I heard about an on-campus stadium. It was a harbinger of things to come. Little did I suspect that Coach Briles would bring unprecedented success to Baylor football, winning two Big 12 championships, recruiting future Heisman Trophy winner Robert Griffin III, and building a top-ten program. Ultimately, however, he—along with Baylor's fourteenth president—would be sacked by Baylor's Board of Regents.

ATHLETIC UPHEAVALS

On-campus stadium issues would have to wait. What was instead lying in wait in Kansas City was a conference-wide question—the very future of the fractious Big 12.

After pulling into the Intercontinental Hotel driveway with Toby Barnett, a senior Baylor fundraiser, I nearly jumped out of the car to tackle the great Tom Osborne, former Cornhuskers football coach, one-time member of Congress, and now Nebraska's athletic director. Coach Osborne was headed into the hotel. Maybe I could catch up with him to introduce myself and say a brief hello. This was far from Malibu-style star-spotting; I greatly admired leaders in college sports, and I held Coach Osborne in particularly high esteem. I was eager to come into his orbit.

While that would soon happen, the orbit immediately proved to be, institutionally, an unstable one. At this conference meeting, the existential issue erupted. Bill Powers, president of UT-Austin, was chairing the session (the chair rotates among the Big 12 members). Bill asked the leaders of each university to speak up about their institution's commitment to the future of the Big 12. Speaking for Texas, he said, "We're in." But there was a soft caveat: "If Nebraska is in." So there it was. Behind the scenes, Nebraska had sent signals that they were shopping for a new home—specifically, as we would later learn, the Big Ten.

One by one around the long rectangular table, the leaders spoke. Most institutions pledged allegiance. Colorado waffled. Nebraska's turn came toward the end of our round robin. NU Chancellor Harvey Perlman, the school's CEO, essentially passed the gavel to his legendary AD. Coach Osborne, in a matter-of-fact tone, said, "I understood the Big Eight. I'm not sure I understand the Big 12." With that comment, the conference realignment earthquake had officially started.

That evening, the presidents and chancellors gathered for a private dinner. No real shop talk, mostly social. Happily, I found myself seated next to Bowen Loftin, Texas A&M's president, a bow-tie aficionado and respected physicist. He spoke a bit ominously: "Ken, I think Baylor should think about the SEC. Texas A&M and Baylor have a lot in common."

Bowen identified the fatal flaw, as he saw it, in the Big 12's structure: inequality. The unequal division of conference revenue was, to Bowen, an enormous, deeply divisive issue. Bowen noted that in the more enlightened SEC, even lowly Vanderbilt—with its frequently losing football seasons—got the exact same revenue distribution as perennial powers such as Alabama's Crimson Tide and the Tigers of LSU. That egalitarian approach, he opined, contributed greatly to the SEC's rock-solid unity and stability. In the Big 12, UT stood as the enormous stumbling block to achieving SEC-style harmony.

I was new on the scene, but I fully understood my modest role: to speak up on behalf of Big 12 unity, to work from within to resolve the issues dividing us, and to help cajole potential deserters to remain in the fold. But Texas's caveat about Nebraska loomed large in my thinking. And it looked as if the Cornhuskers were headed for the exits. So, too— although much less significantly in terms of conference stability—were the Buffalos of Colorado.

Could the conference survive such departures? The Big 12 would suddenly be down to ten members. Where would suitable replacements— especially for Nebraska's vaunted football program—be found?

But exit both schools did, to loud applause in their respective states. Meanwhile, the Longhorns, especially with their menacing new television network, were at least indirectly prompting others to find new conference homes.

Happily, the Longhorns themselves didn't bolt, though it was clear they'd be delighted to consider other platforms, especially the Pac-10. The Pac-10's entrepreneurial commissioner, Larry Scott, was on the prowl, and the conference quickly brought in Colorado, which had a more natural geographic and alumni affinity with California than with Middle America. Utah joined the Pac-10 as well.

Two gone, others unhappy. The future of the Big 12 was, at best, uncertain. Would the Longhorns also walk, perhaps going the route of Notre Dame and Brigham Young universities, and declare themselves independent? Speculation ran rampant, day after day.

The conference agreement imposed heavy exit fees if an institution bolted during the course of the existing agreement. Then again, these were primarily state institutions, and could in theory (and perhaps in real life) assert complete immunity from lawsuits. Could a state university simply tear up the agreement and hide behind the formidable shield of sovereign immunity? The issue hadn't been tested. No one knew the answer, nor was eager to go into litigation to find out.

In short order, and with the help of a professional mediator, the conference agreed on departure terms for both the Cornhuskers and the Buffalos. (Having a law degree, I was appointed to the conference's three-person committee to negotiate these terms, along with Bowen Loftin of A&M and our committee chairman, Burns Hargis of Oklahoma State.)

The Big 12's future grew more uncertain. The next year, Missouri and Texas A&M—ancient rivals of the Baylor Bears—left the conference for the SEC. Bowen Loftin's whisper in Kansas City about the SEC had quickly turned into a cruel reality. Happily, Baylor's archrival TCU and the Mountaineers of West Virginia were eager to join the conference. Big 12 membership would remain at ten.

In the meantime, the conference voted unanimously to embrace equal revenue sharing. That huge, long-overdue reform lifted the terrible pall hanging over the conference. Stability now reigned supreme, buttressed by a lucrative new television contract with two major television partners, ESPN and Fox.

Now the challenge was where it rightly belonged—on the playing fields and arenas of competition. Art Briles and Baylor coaches from the other sports were up to the challenge. Baylor was now a rock-solid member of the reconstructed Big 12; its athletic programs entered a golden era of unprecedented success.

ACADEMIC LEADERSHIP

College athletics should not be the tail that wags the academic dog. But for a wet-behind-the-ears rookie, the cluster of issues swirling around and in intercollegiate athletics—including, most pressingly, conference realignment—was both urgent and important (to draw from Steven Covey's famous quadrant). Athletics constitute what we frequently dub the university's front porch. That's what the world sees from the outside looking in. Athletics, especially football, also unifies the campus and the extended university communities. Controversy rages over whether athletics are too big a deal these days, or whether the money-ball nature of intercollegiate athletics means that student athletes should be paid. (They should not.)

For me, myriad questions emerged from the boiling cauldron of contemporary big-time athletics. My hot-water baptism was underway.

With athletics ever on the front burner, I turned back

to a question of increasingly compelling interest to our thousand-member faculty, and in particular to deans, heads of centers and institutes, and departmental chairs. Who would be Baylor's next chief academic officer? Recent instability and turnover in the provost's position mirrored the topsy-turvy nature of the president's office. Like the CEOs to whom they reported, Baylor provosts came and then soon went away. No university in the country had experienced such turnover at the top—in both the president's and the provost's positions. That was unfortunate, to put it mildly. I fully understood that the stakes were high. This needed to be done right.

At Baylor, the position of provost is impressively styled Executive Vice President and Provost. That means the provost is not only the university's chief academic officer, but also clearly second in command under the president. Yet, the organizational chart in practice seemed a bit uncertain. Exactly who reported to whom? Did all vice presidents report to the second in command? That would seem logical. In practice, however, all the vice presidents reported to the president; only some reported also to the EVP-provost.

Wisely or no, I accepted that ambiguous arrangement, especially in light of the round-table structure and culture I inherited. In particular, the operation of the Executive Council figured prominently in my relationship with the Board of Regents leadership.

Every Friday morning, in Suite 100 of historic Pat Neff Hall, the Executive Council of Vice Presidents (plus the athletic director and general counsel) gathered together with the president and the president's chief of staff. This council devoted the entire morning to issues of the day, great and small. Happily, the EVP-provost was a regular member of this egalitarian round table, a physical structure which fostered a healthy model of collegial collaboration. That works well for universities (though perhaps not for businesses, where no concept of "shared governance" with stakeholders exists). I loved the round table, especially since everyone got along well. In view of that culture of collegiality, a wise and discerning EVP-provost wouldn't try to lord it over lesser-titled colleagues.

As legendary CBS news anchor Walter Cronkite would say at the close of his evening newscasts, "And that's the way it is." The structure I inherited was sound, one that encouraged the open exchange of ideas. No one needed to be shy or timorous; to the contrary, everyone was welcome to speak his or her mind. No one ruled the roost. The metaphor of the legendary Arthurian Round Table was powerful and apt, and seemed congruent with what I was already thinking of as "the Baylor Way." Like Camelot, however, this well-settled structure was destined not to last.

When I arrived at Baylor on June 1, 2010, Elizabeth Davis was occupying the post of acting EVP-provost. Now president of Furman University, Elizabeth was (and is) brilliant. A native of New Orleans, Elizabeth had come to Baylor as an undergrad, majored in computer science, didn't like it, and switched to accounting. Her academic bent illustrated one of her strong qualities: a powerful analytical mind. Elizabeth had graduated from Baylor with high distinction, gone home to New Orleans and toiled in the vineyards of public accounting for a few years (thus tasting life in the real world), then followed her dream to teach. Off to Duke she went for her PhD, where she met fellow doctoral accounting student Charles Davis. Graduate school can be as challenging socially as academically, so their romance made for joyous years in Durham. Married, and with their doctorates in hand, both Elizabeth and Charles headed westward to Baylor to join the Hankamer Business School's already impressive accounting department. Elizabeth and Charles excelled in the classroom and in scholarship.

In due course, Charles rose through the ranks to chair the accounting department. Soon, Elizabeth—thanks to her analytical, numbers-crunching prowess—was tapped to join the provost's office, where she performed brilliantly. When the dizzying Baylor carousel spun off yet another provost, Elizabeth became the acting EVP-provost.

"Acting" is just that. It doesn't mean the temporary occupant is destined for the permanent role. That was, indeed, the big question. Do we launch a nationwide search, which would be entirely appropriate and consistent with industry practice, or do we put up a "Permanent" sign on Elizabeth's office door? (Permanent, that is, by the understandably transient standards of university life.)

I referred earlier to Steve Sample's wise guidance for leaders to engage in artful listening. That's exactly what I did. Listening long and hard, asking the pertinent questions. Before long, it became happily evident that Elizabeth was deeply respected by the faculty, beginning with the deans who reported to her and with department chairs (who report to their respective deans). The heads of centers and institutes (such as Baylor's magnificent Institute for the Study of Religion and the mission-deepening Institute of Faith and Learning) also reported directly to the chief academic officer. To a person, these campus leaders of the university's intellectual and scholarly life praised Elizabeth's on-the-job performance.

In particular, two qualities stood out. Elizabeth listened carefully, and she acted decisively. This listen-and-decide process occurred in the vital context of being superbly prepared for decision-triggering meetings. As she had as a student, Elizabeth always completed her homework, and did it well. One campus leader memorably described the process: "You better be prepared when you go into a meeting with Elizabeth Davis, or—" The sentence didn't need to be completed with "she'll eat your lunch" or whatever. Elizabeth had New Orleans charm and a wry sense of humor, but was also blessed with the proverbial steel-trap mind.

Decisiveness can be an underrated quality. Especially in academic life, it's altogether natural for administrators to sit and stew over a particular matter that should be resolved promptly. This dawdling tendency is by no means unique to university life, of course; in any field, the task of a leader is, in no small part, to lead by deciding, and hopefully inspiring. As a superbly trained and skilled accountant, Elizabeth went about deciding in an orderly and logical way, but also in a highly collaborative manner.

Where were her weaknesses? We all can improve, so where in that broad category of potential self-improvement were Elizabeth's nonstrengths? I perceived only one—her persona at the podium in public speaking contexts. She tended to read her comments, which of course was easy as pie to remedy.

All things considered, she was the logical choice to occupy the permanent role of EVP-provost. So it was that she became the first woman in Baylor's history to take that all-important post. I liked that. As a thirtysomething, I'd cut my teeth back in the Reagan Administration in helping identify and vet Sandra Day O'Connor as the nation's first woman to serve on the highest court in the land. Elizabeth would now break Baylor's version of the glass ceiling.

I also saw her as my own logical successor as president when the time came, as it surely would.

HELPING STUDENTS FINANCIALLY

Without students, a university is only a think tank. With students, a university becomes a community of learning and discovery. From the first university in medieval Bologna, Italy to its twenty-first century manifestations around the world, the university has gathered together faculty members in various disciplines to welcome students who come alongside the faculty and become not only learners but co-discoverers. They also pay the bills.

Eager to connect with students—who energize, inspire, and otherwise "light my bulb"—I eagerly sought out and listened to student leaders (artfully, I hope). Spending time with students, whether in my office or elsewhere around campus, quickly became my favorite part of the day.

In particular, I fell in love with a sixty-year-old Baylor tradition, Dr Pepper Hour, held on Tuesday afternoons in the quaint and cozy Barfield Drawing Room, sweetened by Blue Bell ice cream combined with Dr Pepper in enormous buckets of Dr Pepper floats. With floats in hand, the conversations would begin with basic questions—What year are you? Where are you from? What's your major? When talk turned to hopes, dreams, aspirations, and ambitions, invariably an unhappy subject would emerge: the daunting challenge of high tuition.

The cost of higher education in America was no stranger to Baylor's student ranks. The issue is ubiquitous, save for the abundantly blessed students (less than ten percent of the undergraduate student body) whose family can afford to pay the entire freight. (Even those students of means were frequently rewarded with merit-based scholarship aid.) Indeed, the business plan upon which the compellingly important twenty-first-century Vision 2012 was founded was nothing other than significantly increased tuition and fees. Students would pay for the New Baylor, following decades in which Old Baylor had charged bargain-basement rates for tuition and fees.

This deep-seated student concern was expressed early on in campus meetings. Stories of financial hardship abounded. One story made the point plain as day: "I've been very blessed to be here at Baylor, but my parents simply couldn't make it work for my two younger siblings who also wanted to be Baylor Bears." Here she was, a winsome, attractive, sure-to-succeed student body leader, but her younger brother and sister had to attend lower-tuition institutions. Sure, by God's grace and hard work, the doors of opportunity open regardless of where one goes to college. But I viewed it as a moral imperative to do whatever I could to help those who wanted to attend Baylor to make their dream come true.

We thus launched—with enthusiastic approval from the Board of Regents—the President's Scholarship Initiative. I wanted big. I wanted bold. However, the experts in our development office, whose expertise I rightly trusted, said, "Aim realistically." The idea in fundraising is to set your money goals ambitiously while keeping your feet firmly on the ground. Be judicious. In biblical terms, "Be wise as serpents, harmless as doves." For example, to go hog-wild by trumpeting, "We're today launching a $500-million campaign for scholarships" would be a sure-fire recipe for failure, if not disaster. My colleagues in development were right. Combining the science and art of fundraising, we identified $100 million as the ambitious but realistic goal, to be achieved over a three-year period.

The regents also added a helpful dash of wisdom to the proposed project. Instead of calling the scholarship effort a "campaign," the regents suggested a different label. Calling it an "initiative" would distinguish the money-for-scholarships project from a broader, multipurpose "campaign." Spot on.

We launched the initiative in the early fall of 2010, embarking on this journey entirely by faith.

The rulebook for fundraising sagely counsels such an endeavor should be publicly launched only in the wake of a successful "silent" phase, where a significant portion (say, 30 to 40 percent) of the ultimate goal is in hand, in cash or pledges. We threw the rulebook away. Like the proverbial ticket, "Good for this train and this train only," we ventured out into Baylor Nation and urged alumni and friends and parents to rally around the green-and-gold flag. Please help our students. Do what you can within your means.

Controversially, we raised the minimum amount for an endowed scholarship from $25,000 to $50,000. In doing so, we fully recognized that this would potentially discourage some generously minded potential donors, even with less-demanding installment plans (say, paying an annual contribution over a five-year period). But we needed to step up the level of support. Plus, a $25,000 scholarship would generate only a modest $1,250 annual payout (at an industry-standard 5 percent level).

Baylor Nation responded generously. The largest initial

gift was a million dollars from brand-new board member (and future chairman) Richard Willis and his wife, Karen. Richard had a great story. Growing up in Idaho, he was motivated to come to Baylor by legendary football Coach Grant Teaff's inspiring autobiography, *I Believe*. The son of an academic, Richard majored in business at Baylor, and he'd done well in life. The seven-figure gift from the Willises portended success for the President's Scholarship Initiative overall.

The initiative met with wild enthusiasm. Folks of modest means were motivated to do what they could to help students, with gifts of approximately $100 being the norm. We made it clear as we reached out to the Baylor family: Give what you can. Give biblically, cheerfully, and within your means. We didn't ask for sacrificial giving, though we did lift up the poignant biblical example of the widow lauded by Jesus for her small but highly sacrificial gift to the temple treasury. That was, as we saw it, the Baylor Way.

Responding to the call, Baylor Bears gave in unprecedented numbers, many for the first time. The enthusiasm was contagious. The President's Scholarship Initiative not only proved successful, with over $100 million added to the university's endowment coffers, but served as a harbinger of a vitally important, continuing effort— to encourage Baylor Bears near and far to come alongside their alma mater (including those adopting Baylor in the Alumnus/Alumna by Choice program) through financial support, giving whatever they could.

It worked. Baylor Nation was soon destined to give at historically high levels, both to capital projects and to endowment (scholarships, faculty chairs, and other academic initiatives). The university's total endowment inched toward $1 billion, then a tad beyond. That move upward was destined to help literally thousands of Baylor students make their way through college financially, with reduced debt levels at the end of their educational journey.

For my part, I slept better at night. But this was no time to rest on laurels. Challenges loomed large. As the old song of the church goes, "Work for the night is coming." At times, it seemed as if there was (as the Arthur Koestler book title has it) darkness at noon.

4

CHALLENGES

FOR DECADES, THE BAYLOR ALUMNI ASSOCIATION HAD SERVED AS a university watchdog. BAA's official charter called for it to serve traditional alumni association roles, including providing services to alums around the country (and indeed the world) and contributing to student scholarship funds. But the BAA had taken on a different role, especially in connection with the Vision 2012-inspired transformation under the leadership of President Robert Sloan.

BAA members were, in effect, the loyal opposition. Their role, as key members envisioned it, was to be an outside watchdog ready to blow the whistle on the university's administration—especially the Board of Regents—if Baylor began pursuing a policy or agenda with which the BAA's leadership disagreed.

Disagree they did. Emphatically.

For starters, the BAA was up in arms about the sudden surge in tuition. The hefty hikes were staggering. Sticker shock had set in near and far throughout Baylor Nation. All of a sudden, this hallowed institution was no longer your grandparent's or parent's Baylor. But therein lay the rub; tuition hikes provided the fuel for Baylor's expansion into the world of high-stakes, high-performing higher ed.

This, in short, was the business plan. The ways and means for financing the ambitious Vision 2012 project—

which in time would usher Baylor into the ranks of comprehensive research universities—would be driven, regrettably, by tuition. The boiling hot issue was whether that transformational project would at day's end prove to be a cruel Faustian bargain. Under the skeptical viewpoint, Baylor was turning its back on its history, including accessibility to God-fearing families of modest means, and thus selling its soul in order to lay claim to the ephemeral (and not easily achieved) high research status.

From my perspective, these strongly felt concerns were entirely reasonable. No a priori argument compelled Baylor to become a "me too" research institution, especially in light of its uncompromising Christian commitment. Baylor was about transforming lives, not about Nobel prizes in science or medicine. After all, hadn't ancient Israel fallen into strategic error when, looking to its pagan neighbors, the "We the People" of the Holy Land demanded a constitutional revolution in the form of a king. Judges, like the wise Samuel, had served the chosen people very well indeed. But that was so retro. Israel, the people demanded, needed to enter the "modern era." Monarchy, yes, wise judges, no. Then, and only then, will we be mirroring our neighbors.

A SHOUTING MATCH

One of the glories of American higher education is the extraordinary diversity of institutions, which enjoy freedom (within the broadest limits) to define their own missions. Not everyone needs to be, or aspire to be, Harvard or Cal Berkeley. Why, after all, do we rightly boast about our local community colleges and our homegrown liberal arts colleges? They'll never be a first-tier institution, but so what? As the song from *West Side Story* proclaims, "There's a place for us, somewhere a place for us." That's the very nature of American higher ed. Not one size fits all.

In the United States, college students are blessed with a cafeteria-like array of choices. Some fine institutions such as community colleges (which educate almost half of the American college population), are low-cost providers. Others, like Baylor and Notre Dame, have a more distinctive mission.

Like many faculty members and students, I was drawn to Baylor by its unwavering commitment to quality teaching and research in addition to educating students for "worldwide leadership and service by integrating academic excellence and Christian commitment within a caring community"—to quote Baylor's longstanding mission statement.

One of the glories of democratic societies, where political freedom includes the bedrock liberty to speak one's mind (within very broad limits), is the culture of civil discourse. Chief Justice Warren E. Burger, a stolid Minnesotan for whom I was privileged to serve as a law clerk, expressed it this way: "We need to be able to disagree with one another without being disagreeable." Rightly said. One of the reasons I asked Professor Stephen Carter of the Yale Law School to serve as keynoter at my inauguration ceremony (by happy coincidence, held on Constitution Day, September 17, 2010) was my admiration for his splendid book entitled *Civility*. But the world in the twenty-first century had become decidedly uncivil. My dear friend Gordon Gee, president of West Virginia University, astutely opined that in this new century, "The world has become a shouting match." The presidential election of 2016 confirmed that unhappy truth.

Tragically, the deep-seated differences over Vision 2012 between the university administration—supported by the Board of Regents—and the BAA devolved into just such a shouting match among the Baylor community. Perfectly reasonable differences of opinion became infected with bitter personality conflicts. It was a toxic, vitriol-filled combo. That's one reason my wise mentor from northern Virginia, Alan Merten, the highly acclaimed, long-serving president of George Mason University (my adopted academic home in the D.C. area), had strongly counseled that I steer clear of the Baylor boiler pot and remain happily ensconced in the more peaceful Santa Monica Mountains.

What to do? As always, the initial step was to listen artfully and try to learn, since the circumstances at Baylor were all new to me. I asked a number of basic questions. Why was an alumni association separate and independent from the university itself? To be sure, that structure made perfect sense for a public institution, both for tax reasons and in order to lawfully permit lobbying efforts. Texas Exes, the gold standard of alumni associations, was fully independent of the University of Texas at Austin, but its mission was indisputably to support and to build the state's flagship university. I was, in truth, unfamiliar with the structure whereby in a private college or university an outside alumni association operated independently of the university. From my perspective, limited as it was by my own narrow set of experiences, that made no sense whatsoever. I said so, from day one. From that initial position, I never wavered.

Ying and yang. At the same time, I had great respect for history and tradition. Each institution obviously has its own DNA, born of its own practical experience. So perhaps the fiercely independent BAA fell into the category of an exception that proves the rule. Perhaps at Baylor, uniquely, there needed to be an alumni association looking in from the outside and serving as a sentinel on the watchtower.

Was it so? Was there something peculiar or unique in Baylor's history to warrant this exception? After all, in my world of law (to which I regularly repaired for analogies), the Fourth Amendment's foundational principle of our liberties as a free people requires a warrant to support a "search" or "seizure." Yet over time, exceptions to the warrant requirement have emerged based on people's experiences; the compelling exigencies of law enforcement as carried out on the streets of America had to be respected.

COURTESY, RESPECT, HOSPITALITY

This was a high-wire act. Some of the regents, including leaders such as Dary Stone and soon-to-be chairman Buddy Jones, a superpowerful Austin lobbyist, had feelings on the subject that went way beyond "strong." Dary was diplomatic, but clear. Buddy was simply clear. The BAA had to be destroyed.

Almost immediately, I convened an informal council of advisers as a working group. I asked these loyal, dedicated alumni to focus on key issues of current interest and concern. In effect, I created a sounding board—and a buffer—with respect to hot-button issues relating to the BAA. I wanted wisdom, to be sure, but I also needed cover.

I soon had it. As we sat around the round table in Pat Neff Hall, I probed various issues with this splendid group of Baylor savants, but none of the issues rose to the level of what to do vis-à-vis the BAA. Extemporaneously, a wise Houston lawyer, Joe Coleman, said this: "The BAA is an important group. They have strong support. Whatever the right answer ultimately, I recommend that you treat the alumni association with courtesy, respect, and hospitality."

Bingo. I wrote down the words. They were kind, gracious, and deeply Christian. They echoed through the channels of memory—of time out of mind.

Hospitality is a defining characteristic of good manners, but more deeply, it evokes principles of basic respect and fundamental human dignity. Out of Joe Coleman's musings, I had my bumper sticker that captured and conveyed university policy toward the BAA. More importantly, I had an inspired articulation of an animating principle. The goal was clear and admirable: We would work to bring the BAA in-house, hopefully sooner rather than later, and eventually to consolidate the entire alumni-relations function with university operations. After all, as I saw it, we needed to pull together as a Baylor family, especially in light of the myriad challenges facing independent institutions of higher education. As I said time and again, "We all need to get in the same boat and row in the same direction."

I announced the policy—courtesy, respect, and hospitality—to the full Board of Regents at their homecoming meeting in October 2010. To their great credit, the regents listened respectfully. Their body language seemed supportive. Whatever the battles of yesteryear, we seemed within Baylor Nation to be entering a period of peaceful coexistence.

I was wrong.

PATIENCE AND HARD FEELINGS

Quite apart from the rancor and acrimony of recent years, the BAA was severely handicapped in its wannabe role as *the* alumni organization for the entire Baylor family (other than the alumni association which is an integral part of the fabled Baylor Law School). The first handicap was the limited scale and scope of the BAA's services. One of my pet peeves was the splendid but woefully limited set of offerings in Baylor's continuing education (or lifelong learning). Nothing was to be found online, nor were courses offered in cities other than Waco. To partake of this enrichment opportunity, using Baylor's magnificent faculty, the lifelong learner essentially needed to retire to the banks of the Brazos. Good idea, and lots of Baylor alums did just that, but this was of course utterly impractical for the overwhelming majority of grads spread to the four winds.

The BAA was also hamstrung by a flinty structural reality. As a membership organization, the BAA needed members to pony up to support the organization and pay the bills. I fundamentally disagreed with that model. As I saw it, alumni services are better conceived—and provided—as part and parcel of what a college or university offers, unless legal restrictions or prohibitions prevent full integration into the university's infrastructure. Due to its membership dependency, the BAA could legitimately lay claim to only a small fraction of the entire Baylor alumni community. Specifically, the BAA claimed some 20,000 members. (The number varied from time to time, but in no event was the association's total membership higher than 10 percent or so of the entire Baylor alumni family numbering more than 170,000.)

Second, the BAA services, such as continuing education and homecoming activities, tended to be focused geographically on Waco and the surrounding area. That might have sufficed in the halcyon days of yore, but not in the Global Century. The exception to this geographically limited service area was the BAA's widely read publication *The Baylor Line,* effectively distributed far and wide to BAA members wherever they might be.

Slowly, through continued cooperation and mutual agreement, the BAA's service functions peacefully were brought "in house" to the university's growing and vibrant Division of Constituent Engagement headed by Tommye Lou Davis, the iconic and energetic master teacher from the Classics Department, and the cohost for Alice back in the spring of 2010 during the future first lady's under-the-radar exploratory visit to the banks of the Brazos.

TLou, as she's affectionately known, was tapped early on during my tenure to head up this division and provide a robust set of services not only for alumni but also for affinity groups such as the increasingly important category of Baylor parents (regardless of their own alma mater). Thus was born "the Network," which by its very name connotes a deep connection with twenty-first-century modes of operation.

Above all, no dues. Indeed, at every graduation, TLou would conclude the ceremony—immediately prior to the benediction and the traditional singing of "That Good Old Baylor Line"—with the happy announcement that the newly minted grads were now automatically part of the Baylor Network. "We believe you've already paid your dues. Get involved, stay involved, be engaged." This and similar admonitions would flow from TLou at the Ferrell Center podium as literally the last word of congratulatory remarks delivered by the university to the newest members of the fabled Baylor Line.

Patience, patience, patience. Frequently, I counseled colleagues—and myself—to keep moving forward, but not to expect road-to-Damascus experiences in bringing about full integration in the alumni services galaxy. Time, I thought, was on our side. Importantly, more recent Baylor graduates were essentially unaware of the BAA.

Eventually, if we were able consistently to display courtesy, respect, and hospitality, I strongly believed that the preferred model of university-provided alumni/constituent services would carry the day through peaceful evolution. As proof, I cited an organization of alumni officers from around the country. Out of forty private, independent institutions, no fewer than thirty-nine had embraced the integrated, inside-the-university model I was trumpeting.

Baylor was the proverbial odd man out. I freely acknowledged that being out of step with twenty-first-century practice didn't necessarily answer the question of what's the best model for Baylor. But to my thinking, the very fact that everyone except Baylor had embraced the integrated alumni-constituent services approach was highly significant.

We moved forward. The Board of Regents engaged fruitfully and constructively in the effort to achieve integration. Board leaders spent countless hours in discussion and negotiation with BAA's elected leaders, seeking a path forward. Agreement was finally reached between the two boards. When put to a plebiscite, a significant majority (55 percent) voted in favor of integration, but the total fell short of the requisite two-thirds supermajority. Soon thereafter, the university—at my urging and with the Board of Regents' approval—filed suit to prevent the BAA from continuing to use the Baylor name and trademarks.

Meanwhile, as work began on the dazzling new on-campus football stadium, the BAA's gathering place on

University Parks Avenue was slated for demolition. Hughes-Dillard Alumni Center would be torn down to make way for an esplanade connecting the main campus to the Sheila and Walter Umphrey pedestrian bridge over the Brazos, leading to the new stadium.

One day I found myself on a campus driving tour at the request of Jim Vardaman, a Baylor alum and a retired master teacher. With Jim at the wheel, we headed to the expansive parking lot of the Ferrell Center and motored over to where the Brazos flows by. Bountifully growing riverbank foliage completely obstructed the scenic river below. "This needs to be cut down," Jim opined.

I readily agreed. "I'll call Ian McCaw," I offered. I was confident our can-do AD would get the job done.

Our campus journey continued. We ventured westward on University Parks toward I-35 and pulled slowly past Hughes-Dillard. "Do not cut this down," Jim stated emphatically. "If you do, you'll leave wounds for an entire generation."

Hughes-Dillard represented the single largest obstacle to peace and unity within the Baylor family. But down it came.

To say that bitterness resulted would be a gross understatement. Litigation ensued over whether demolition was absolutely necessary. In short order, the judicial order temporarily halting the demolition was lifted, and Hughes-Dillard came down. But hard feelings—very hard—remained. They remain so to this day.

Peace

Even with this barrier to unity, however, a peace process launched by fiercely loyal Baylor double alumnus Ed Kinkeade, a United States District Judge in Dallas, finally bore fruit. On the foundation laid by Judge Kinkeade and Baylor Law School's accomplished and energetic dean, Brad Toben, steady, patient work was applied by Richard Willis as board chairman and by Cary Gray, a leading Houston lawyer and Baylor regent.

Within the Baylor family, conflict subsided. The BAA, to its credit, voluntarily reorganized itself as the Baylor Line Foundation, maintaining its independent voice through *The Baylor Line* magazine (plus online messages cleverly entitled "Between the Lines") and focusing on providing student scholarships.

Although quickly lost in the fog of other controversies, particularly the explosive emergence of tragic issues concerning sexual violence and Title IX compliance, a peaceful accord was reached. At long last, the Baylor family stood unified. Alumni outreach efforts are now consolidated in the Baylor Network, under TLou's leadership, while important values of a separate, independent voice were preserved.

The wall of division had at long last come down. Even if hard feelings remained over the destruction of Hughes-Dillard, the ever-growing family of Baylor alumni had joined hands. Blessed are the peacemakers.

5

OPPORTUNITIES

THE "UNI" IN UNIVERSITY SIGNALS ONENESS. UNITY. BUT WHAT DOES organic chemistry or quantum physics share in common with poli-sci or history? In general, various academic disciplines—with new ones emerging, such as environmental science or neuroscience—are siblings within the broad family of human knowledge and understanding, a family which continually expands as it pursues human flourishing and well-being. That's a high-level but nonetheless practical yardstick for measuring the value of an arena of inquiry. In Christian higher education, an overarching theological lens is added through which the value proposition of a particular project or initiative is viewed.

A real example of this is a proposal at Baylor to create a joint degree bringing together theology (Truett Seminary) and social work (the Diana Garland School of Social Work)—an MDiv and an MSW. The noble concept—bringing together theological training for ministry and expertise in social work—would (and did) pass with flying colors. Or indeed, the creation of the seminary in the first instance. Or the Garland School itself, growing out of a department within a broader college.

The basic question is posed again and again: How can our university—as one institution with many members or constituents—serve the cause of human understanding and human flourishing?

This train of thought led to the creation and launch of what we dubbed the Washington Initiative. Geographically, Baylor—deep in the heart of Texas—is fifteen hundred miles removed from the country's center of power and policy. But what galvanized the university's leadership—including a unanimously supportive Board of Regents—toward Washington D.C. was the challenge and opportunity of religious liberty.

Georgetown University, the crown jewel of Jesuit institutions of higher education, sits atop scenic bluffs overlooking the Potomac, twenty blocks northwest of the White House in Washington. Its history predates America's seat of government in the District of Columbia.

Under the broad Georgetown University umbrella resides the Religious Freedom Project (RFP) of the Berkley Center. By virtue of the growing friendship between Byron Johnson of Baylor's Institute for the Studies of Religion, and the two key leaders of Georgetown's RFP, Tom Farr and Tim Shah, Baylor launched the Washington Initiative.

This was one of my close-to-the-heart projects. Now, more than ever, religious freedom finds itself on the barricades in American cultural and political life. Beyond our borders, pressure points have been increasing around the globe. Baylor needed to stand up and be heard. Partnering with the RFP, and vicariously luxuriating in the global prestige of Georgetown, represented a golden opportunity. We jumped at the chance.

And how fitting and proper, as Mr. Lincoln would say. As the world's largest Baptist university, Baylor belonged to a rich and cherished history in supporting the right of all persons, everywhere, to enjoy religious freedom and freedom of conscience. Baptist contributions to the culture of religious liberty have been broad and wide.

The Baptist commitment to religious liberty was grounded theologically and philosophically in the idea and ideal of "soul competency." Fiercely nonhierarchical, the Baptist polity was one of shared commitment to a biblical vision of individual accountability to God. That individuality translated into the ability to interpret Scripture for oneself. No interpreting intermediary or guide was needed. Steep oneself in Scripture, and use one's God-given abilities and insights to determine one's course.

This individualistic outlook had political ramifications when this nation was founded, as Baptists flocked to the anti-establishment ranks of Jeffersonian anti-Federalists. John Adams's Federalist perspective, in contrast, had deep roots in the established clergy of New England, with their established churches, which had been protected to a greater or lesser extent by state authority.

All this was behind Baylor's bracing partnership with Georgetown. The Baptist individualistic perspective added a richness to the more philosophical and communitarian reflections informing Georgetown's commitment to individual freedom. The marriage was unofficially blessed by Pope Francis in an inspiring conference in the Vatican in late 2013. The Washington Initiative was launched in sacred space.

The public roll-out of this initiative came in March 2014. As befits an academic enterprise of this sort, the Washington Initiative was unveiled with food and fellowship, but undergirded by substantive discussions. Following a splendid lunch at the Willard Hotel on Pennsylvania Avenue, I participated in a two-way, unmoderated conversation with Alan Dershowitz, the brilliant and recently retired Harvard law professor. Our discussion was about religious freedom against the backdrop of the Hobby Lobby case, which was to be argued the next day in the Supreme Court.

The case was highly controversial and hard-fought. A deeply divided Court of Appeals in Denver had narrowly ruled in favor of the government's position that the Affordable Care Act, through administrative rulings, could constitutionally require all covered employers to provide various forms of contraceptive services, including those viewed by conscientious objectors as abortifacients.

This was quintessential grist for the Washington Initiative mill—to foster and deepen understanding about the busy intersection where government regulation clashed with deeply held religious beliefs. In the Hobby Lobby case specifically, the owners of the privately held Hobby Lobby firm objected to the company's being required to provide four of the twenty specified forms of reproductive preventive services; these four were regarded by Hobby Lobby's owners as abortion-like procedures.

Such a gravely serious issue merited serious discussion. We accomplished that goal. The debate was conducted civilly, with shared respect for each other's viewpoints. The precise question was the reach of the Religious Freedom Restoration Act of 1993, passed by a unanimous House of Representatives and an overwhelming 97-3 vote in the Senate, then enthusiastically signed into law by President Bill Clinton. The argument—which eventually carried the day with a five-to-four vote of the Supreme Court—was that the federal government had adequate alternative means of reaching its goals for the Affordable Care Act without riding roughshod over religious freedoms guaranteed by the U.S. Constitution and the Religious Freedom Restoration Act.

A primary architect of the Religious Freedom Restoration Act had been U.S. Rep. Frank Wolf, a tireless evangelical Christian. Retiring from Congress after serving seventeen consecutive terms, he became one of the pillars of Baylor's Washington Initiative. Frank's well-deserved title: the Jerry and Susie Wilson Chair in Religious Freedom. Through the generosity of the Wilsons, Frank had what he eagerly desired—a place where he could influence young lives, who in turn would impact the culture. His visits each semester to Baylor's campus, where he lectured to student audiences large and small, were inspiring to all of us— and in particular to student organizations that lifted up the overarching value of human freedom and freedom of conscience.

At the heart of the Washington Initiative was the mission-furthering role of Waco-based faculty and the simultaneous creation of study-and-work opportunities for Baylor's students in the nation's capital. We never tired of saying: "It's all about the students!" Religious freedom and freedom of conscience were organizing themes that set the Baylor initiative in Washington apart.

The structure quickly fell into place, thanks to the labors of Dean Tom Hibbs of the Honors College and Byron Johnson, the UPenn criminologist who answered the Vision 2012 call to come to Baylor and found the Institute for the Study of Religion. Dean Hibbs, previously chair of the philosophy department at Boston College and founding dean of the Honors College at Baylor, brought to the Washington Initiative both vast learning and show-stopping erudition, impressively combined with a feet-on-the-ground common sense. He was deeply admired in Chestnut Hill.

Steeped in both the ancients and medieval philosophy, Dean Hibbs nonetheless spoke eloquently into contemporary culture. *National Review*, one of my favorite periodicals, often featured his wide-ranging reviews of movies and books. Brilliant, winsome, and a deeply devoted Catholic, he was a modern-day "man for all seasons."

Dean Hibbs also proved to be a great negotiator. In warp-like speed, he hammered out a proposed agreement with American University to permit Baylor students to live on the beautiful Wesley Heights campus, take courses at AU, and yet pay comparatively bargain-basement tuition levels. (It bears noting that Baylor's lofty tuition levels are nonetheless dwarfed by those at private institutions on the East and West Coasts, including American University.)

For his part, Byron Johnson remained our ambassador extraordinaire to and liaison with Georgetown, and in particular to Berkley Center leaders Tom Farr and Tim Shah. Whenever issues arose between our two institutions, Byron was there to iron them out. He's by nature a builder, with his soft-spoken, confidence-building manner augmented by his native Tennessee charm.

These two—Byron and Tom—were the perfect twosome to make good things happen for Baylor in the nation's capital. And that included the third leg of the Washington Initiative: faculty engagement.

We brought Baylor faculty members to Washington each month during the academic year for riveting programs and presentations featuring our enormously impressive array of faculty talent. One example is a faculty panel on C. S. Lewis before a standing-room-only audience; another is an inspiring lecture by Professor Lori Baker, a forensic anthropologist whose work in reuniting families on the U.S.-Mexico border has won plaudits from virtually countless humanitarian and civic causes. Accompanied by Baylor students, and employing state-of-the-art forensic methodology, Professor Baker and her team would identify human remains of tragic border crossings and then bring closure to anxious families in Mexico or elsewhere in Latin America who were awaiting word about the fate of their loved ones who'd sought a better life in America.

Baylor students in D.C. were of course encouraged to attend the various presentations there from Baylor faculty, and thus come into the orbit of Baylor alums living in and around Washington. Waco-D.C. connections steadily increased.

Baylor students were prized additions to D.C. offices, including on Capitol Hill. Refreshingly, up-and-coming Baylor Bears were not only intelligent and hard-working, they exhibited good character and a charming Texas-friendly demeanor that endeared them to the grizzled veterans of capital wars where politics is notoriously a blood sport. The students made us proud. Some would decide to make their careers in the federal government; others enthusiastically learned and served, but headed home inspired by the idea of serving the American people in other ways.

That's the Baylor Way. After all, Judge Baylor himself

had served in the U.S. House of Representatives. Six generations later, Baylor students who studied and labored in the nation's capital under the auspices of the Washington Initiative were destined to follow in the founder's large footsteps.

6

STUDENTS

THROUGHOUT THE SUMMER EACH YEAR, "SEND-OFF PARTIES" ACROSS the country bring together incoming Baylor freshmen (joined by parents and loved ones) with returning Baylor students living and working in that area. Typically, a send-off party is hosted in a home; in some instances, the host family continues extending this welcome-to-Baylor hospitality long after their own student has entered Baylor's alumni ranks.

Reflecting teamwork at its best, these events are overwhelmingly volunteer-driven in planning and execution, although Baylor staff members also attend, especially folks from Constituent Engagement (the office headed by Tommye Lou Davis) and University Development (led by Dave Rosselli).

This Baylor tradition was a summer highlight, and I attended as many send-offs as my schedule permitted. Alice frequently attended on her own, and was always a big hit.

Baylor send-off parties are an early introduction into the Baylor Way. Here's an example from a party I attended, one of the approximately eighty such celebrations held that summer. Also present was standout Baylor athlete Robert Griffin III, who'd won the Heisman Trophy just eight months earlier. RG III had graduated with honors, and in three short years, then continued on (as student athletes frequently are able to do) into graduate school at Baylor.

That summer he was looking ahead to summer training camp as a rookie with the Washington Redskins—and what later turned out to be a magical rookie season. But on that occasion he'd graciously chosen to participate in the Baylor event. The setting was a poolside in a northern Virginia backyard.

After the customary fellowship hour featuring Dr Pepper floats (a Baylor must) and Waco-baked green-and-gold cookies festooned with Baylor's interlocking BU, the incoming freshmen lined up. Each in his or her turn talked about their high school, their prospective major at Baylor, their residence hall, etc.

Then the returning Baylor students came to stand with the freshmen and offer a word of encouragement. Into the line with his fellow students went none other than RG III. His turn came to speak. With admirable humility, he simply said, "I'm Robert Griffin III, and I'm completing my master's degree in communications. My word of advice for the freshmen is this: 'At BU, you can be you.'"

Spot on. And yet, Robert's poolside insight was incomplete. At Baylor, the goal was not simply a continuation of the status quo—to "be you." Our ambitious aspiration was the transformation of student lives, a maturing of the way young men and women looked at the world. Sparked by Vision 2012 and carried on by *Pro Futuris*, the goal was a new person, equipped with marketable skills to be sure, but with a fundamental and critical element—a Christian worldview, an inspired way of looking at all of life. As the mission statement trumpeted, students were being prepared for worldwide leadership and service.

THE BAYLOR WAY

Early Christians were known simply as the Way. The name signaled a radical departure from the old. Baylor's "way" is far from radical, but it is deeply intentional. In its own manner, the Baylor Way of undergraduate education is focused on a highly relational, residential experience, with a strong emphasis on extracurricular engagement, which I viewed as the cauldron of leadership development.

The ideal is the purposeful formation and nurturing of community and an identification of the individual self within the context of that larger community of friends and colleagues. Again, the stated goal, set forth in the longstanding mission statement, is to prepare young women and men for lives of "worldwide leadership and service." As befits the bold ambitions of Baylor's founding generation, that's a tall order. How to execute?

The first transformational principle is shepherded, guided engagement with one's peers. The seeds are planted early on in what's known as Line Camp, put on by Baylor's magnificent Division of Student Life (life, that is, outside the classroom). For the better part of a week during the summer months, cohorts of approximately 220 entering freshmen live together in campus residence halls during an intense period of purpose-filled interaction. Living together in community creates a social bond of enduring power. Lifelong friendships emerge from the long summer days and evenings of learning together through shared projects and activities.

I love Line Camp. Energy pulsates from the eager incoming students, with chants and yells lasting on into the summer evening (but mercifully controlled by mature upperclassmen leaders). Within twenty-four hours, the blest "tie that binds" has been formed, and the initiates are psychologically committed to one another as enthusiastic Baylor Bears. Community forms organically, with impressive speed.

The highlight of the entire experience is a field trip to where the Baylor experiment all began—the tiny village of Independence. A caravan of buses wends southeasterly toward Bryan-College Station, then snake their way single file on state roads to the crossroads that Baylor first called home. The students alight from their buses, tour the village's original Baptist Church, where they hear a stirring lecture on Texas Baptist history and the founding of the university. They enjoy a picnic dinner under the welcome shade of ancient oak trees. They roam around the remains of the Windmill Hill campus (home of young Baylor men), explore the stunningly gorgeous Rose Emporium, then gather for an emotional sunset celebration.

As evening shadows gather, the students stand shoulder to shoulder facing the iconic four columns that still grace beautiful Academy Hill. Familiar hymns are sung, softly, tenderly. A meditation invites the worshipers to reflect on their gifts, to listen to the voice within that points each of the students toward a lifetime goal, a destination. "Ask yourself: What are my gifts? What am I being called to do?" "Jesus came to serve, not to be served. So how can I serve?"

The music concludes, the candles go dark, and single file the Baylor students proceed through the four columns to receive their coveted Baylor Line jerseys—with the year of their projected graduation adorning the back.

The evening in Independence usually concludes with tears, with sweet emotions of deep attachment to an institution and its rich history. On this ground walked

STUDENTS 85

Baylor students, men and women, almost two centuries ago. Here, General Sam Houston watched with parental pride as his daughters received their Baylor education. Here, the executive decision was wisely made to move to Waco.

Then it's back to the waiting buses with running lights beckoning. Farewell to Independence. The comfort of East Village residence halls awaits a hundred miles away, upriver on the Brazos. It will be a good night's sleep after an action-filled morning on campus, capped by this emotion-filled afternoon trip that will vividly live on in memory for a lifetime. The symbolism-rich journey to Independence is the beginning, emotionally and spiritually, of the lifelong journey along the path that's the Baylor Way.

Small wonder that, four years later, graduating seniors jump for the chance to take a sentimental journey (sponsored by TLou's Constituent Engagement Division) back to Independence during "dead week." Moving on soon to their callings discerned or confirmed on a hot summer evening four years previously, the seniors are now to take their own places among proud Baylor alumni around the world.

Line Camp is the portal, psychologically, into Baylor life. It's a deep introduction to the proposition that college, at its best, is lived exuberantly outside the classroom as well as in labs, seminar rooms, and libraries. Line Camp knows no tests nor grades. It's a living laboratory of living life together, including a community service project to round out and enrich the deeply relationship-building experience.

After the exhilarating intensity of Line Camp, freshmen appetites are thoroughly whetted for Welcome Week. Small wonder that retention rates, an important objective yardstick of university success, are significantly higher among Line Camp veterans. Life is about relationships. And Line Camp creates powerful ties among entering freshmen that bind the campers not only to one another but to the entire enterprise of college life. It also instills confidence: "I belong here."

IT'S ABOUT RELATIONSHIPS

Welcome Week for freshmen launches on a Wednesday and concludes on Sunday evening. A lot gets packed into those few days.

Almost three thousand volunteers will ensure that every new student's actual move into the assigned room is painless and bordering on effortless. Within ninety seconds of pulling up to the residence hall, the vehicle (and at times the accompanying U-Haul trailer) will be drained of the freshman's worldly possessions, all carried inside by a veritable horde of students, faculty, administrators, and even community volunteers, each of them wearing message-laden t-shirts supplied by the Division of Student Life. There's plenty of work involved in moving in so quickly over three thousand freshmen (separated by gender, the traditional Baylor Way). Literally hundreds of upperclassmen return early in order to assist in this move-in process. Applied to campus life, this is American volunteerism at its best, a collegiate form of community barn-raising.

That evening, these new freshmen head off into evening shadows, each with his or her previously assigned small group led by an upperclassman. Once again, the message is conveyed: College is much more than the core curriculum, which Baylor proudly trumpets, or dedicating oneself to a major (one or more). It's about relationships.

Baylor alum and donor Drayton McLane, Jr. expressed it well in speaking before leadership seminars and evening gatherings at Truett Seminary's welcoming Great Hall: "At Baylor, I learned much more outside the classroom than I did inside." (Drayton quipped that Herb Reynolds, who served wisely as president over the span of two decades, would remonstrate: "Drayton, stop saying that!" But it was true.)

In similar vein, Ed Crenshaw, a highly successful and recently retired CEO of Publix, a much-respected grocery store chain based in Florida, paid tribute to his experience as president of Student Foundation, a wonderful organization that helps recruit students to Baylor and raises money for scholarships. Serving in this servant-leadership role paved the way, Ed explains, for his highly successful business career.

Happily, well over three hundred student organizations provide abundant opportunities for students to learn, grow, and lead outside the classroom. That's the Baylor Way.

Drayton's and Ed's paean to extracurricular life on the Baylor campus reflects the fundamental principle of Baylor undergraduate education—lives will be transformed through the holistic experience of living and serving in community together. Online learning has its place, but the Baylor Way affirms that learning occurs most fruitfully and enduringly in community together, guided by a faculty member who personally and deeply relates to the student's whole person. Caring deeply for the students means a personal relationship nurtured by actual face-to-face interactions, including invitations into that faculty member's home to break bread and enjoy fellowship.

ONLINE EDUCATION

This is by no means a knock on online learning. Especially for nontraditional students who have work or family obligations, it's likely online education or nothing. Indeed, for so much of the world, in country after country, online education is all there is. All too frequently around the globe, access to traditional university or college life just isn't available.

And thus, the concept of massive online courses is an important one, globally as well as in the United States. Universities are to be heartily commended for providing access to their most towering scholars and teachers.

By way of example, my dear friend Akhil Reed Amar, Sterling Professor of Law and Political Science at Yale, delighted in putting together an online course on America's Constitution. The cost to the student: gratis. This kind of offering is a public service of literally incalculable value to civic education and understanding. It deserves our applause and our gratitude for enriching life and promoting human flourishing.

Back on campus, educational best practices creatively employ online elements through what's dubbed "blended learning." That is, integrating online components or blocs into a traditional course predictably yields abundant fruit. Carnegie Mellon University, a pioneer in online education, conducted a study years ago demonstrating that in the dauntingly challenging course of organic chemistry, learning outcomes improved significantly through skillful employment of online elements, including even lab assignments. At earlier education levels, online learning can provide a spark, a catalyst, to stimulate interest.

Another illustration, drawn from secondary education:

iCivics, an online learning tool championed by retired Justice Sandra Day O'Connor, provides an increasingly popular example. The idea is interactive learning, empowering students to participate in the learning exercise as real actors (say, as a member of Congress or a Supreme Court justice), rather than hew to the venerable (but, alas, outdated) model of lecture halls or crowded classrooms with dedicated teachers—or even learned professors—holding forth for fifty minutes straight. Research carried out by Baylor's School of Education confirmed what Justice O'Connor witnessed firsthand: America's rising generation can engage in deep learning about our system of government through online engagement using iCivics.

To foster the Baylor Way, we must welcome technological tools that make learning more enriching and rewarding.

SPIRITUAL LIFE

Although chapel attendance is required for Baylor freshmen (or at least for one complete academic year of the student's tenure), there's no grade involved. Twice a week, it's show up and log in, then it's up to the student whether he or she will benefit from what unfolds inside iconic Waco Hall.

The Spiritual Life Office, an integral component of the Division of Student Life, is headed by a remarkable, eloquent chaplain with the Baylor-royalty surname of Burleson, who in turn is supported by a small but superb student-centric staff. Chapel is right on target in fostering Baylor's mission—it's unapologetically designed to encourage students' spiritual growth and maturation. Each week, Monday's chapel session is given over entirely to worship; Wednesday's session, in contrast, features a short devotional followed by a presentation from an outside speaker.

At times, the guest speaker proves controversial. Bob Fu, a survivor of the Tiananmen Square massacre and a convert to Christianity, caused a walk-out of students from China when he described the baleful state of religious liberty in his native land. Usually, however—and by design—guest speakers are chosen not to confront but to encourage and inspire.

Here again, outside the traditional classroom or lab, lives are changed. One example: Jim Gash, the multi-talented law prof from Pepperdine. Jim regaled the chapel students (approximately three thousand attendees over the course of three morning sessions) with his story (also told in his page-turner *Divine Collision*). Running away year after year from opportunities to serve the cause of justice in East Africa, Jim finally relented. His life changed on that first trip to Uganda with Pepperdine students and law alums. He saw up close and personal the need for students and profs to go serve, with their talent and skill set, the least of these.

Baylor students were captivated by the story, as well as by Jim's wake-up intro when he put on his college football helmet, took an imaginary hike from a phantom center, faded back into the unseen "pocket," and launched a perfect spiral up into the balcony (a thirty-five-yard picture-perfect pass to a waiting staffer up in the balcony). His message: Sometimes you do your best, but you lose the game. Keep going.

Startup student organizations not infrequently emerge out of chapel presentations, a dynamic, generative process that creates yet more leadership opportunities for upperclassmen—a constant for the Baylor Way. The Division of Student Life has to review and approve the application for official recognition (a customary and appropriate screening mechanism), but permission is freely granted. The International Justice Mission (IJM) student chapter is one of the vibrant justice-seeking and serving organizations that grew like mustard seed out of a chapel presentation by IJM founder Gary Haugen, an occasional visitor to Baylor's campus. Another example: the Baylor Wells Project was born out of a presentation by a representative from the Living Wells ministry, which both educates those of us blessed to live in a land of plenty about the compelling need for clean water and raises money to drill fresh-water wells in at-risk societies.

Chapel presentations are augmented by a steady stream of outside speakers, invited by the university itself or student organizations, who lift up worthy causes and ministries. Above all, students are continually being invited to join in ministry—especially through a discipline-specific mission trip. Student athletes head to Kenya or Zambia or, more recently, Brazil; "Engineers with a Mission" devote themselves to much-needed projects in Central America or Haiti. And for pre-med students (almost one-third of entering freshmen express a vocational interest in health services, including of course the challenging hope of entering medical school), medical mission opportunities summon these future doctors, nurses, and health practitioners to serve those who our Lord lovingly called "the least of these."

This is all part and parcel of the Baylor Way.

CHURCH INVOLVEMENT

These myriad opportunities are augmented by the energetic engagement and involvement of local churches, one of the many jewels that enrich life in and around Waco. Literally hundreds of Baylor students, for example, flock to Antioch Church, where they're inspired to serve as missionaries and church planters both here in the U.S. and around the world. In the summer of this writing, four hundred or so Baylor Bears are fanning out across Europe and serving the needs of Syrian refugees in several European countries, including on the "front lines" in Greece. Other Antioch attendees head annually to Mongolia, of all places, which has embraced the ideals and practices of religious liberty (a cause close to my heart).

Gordon Melton, a renowned sociologist who now calls Baylor's renowned Institute for the Studies of Religion his professional home, estimates that there are more than four hundred churches in and around Waco. That may well be the highest per capita number of churches anywhere in the world.

Not surprisingly, Baylor students emerge from their Waco experience committed to the mission and work of local congregations. Some follow the example of the apostle Paul. A tentmaker by day, Paul was frequently self-supporting even though he could rightly lay claim to the financial support of the young churches that he and his missionary companions had established. Baylor grads will start up a business in unchurched (relatively speaking) communities and contemporaneously plant a new church.

This town-and-gown combination, with Baylor students engaging in local Waco congregational life, has sown virtually countless seeds of ministries and outposts in an increasingly secular culture. That's at the core of the Baylor Way: *pro ecclesia*—for the church; and *pro Texana*—for Texas, a metaphor for the world.

THE GPS

A closing word about the students: each year, I would select two graduating seniors to serve as special assistants for the coming academic year, summer to summer. These were always accomplished student leaders who embodied the Baylor Way—and Baylor's mission—during their respective educational journeys. Each in his or her own way was invaluable. They became not merely assistants but faithful and tireless companions, serving all the while as eagle-eye observers of campus trends from the all-important student perspective.

Because I selected a young woman and young man each year, and since I wasn't terribly fond of the overused term "special assistant," I quickly dubbed my two youthful colleagues as "Gentlepersons." Across campus, they were known with affection as the GPs. No keeper of the political correctness torch could reasonably take offense at that appellation. I pay tribute to them here for their invaluable service to Baylor, and of course to me personally. They're very dear to Uncle Ken (the familiar name by which Baylor students increasingly called their institution's fourteenth president). Their student status now behind them, the GPs have gone on—in myriad ways—to "fling their green and gold afar." They reflect Baylor—and the Baylor Way—at its best.

7

ACADEMICS

WHETHER AT SEND-OFF PARTIES, AT ORIENTATION, DURING Welcome Week, indeed at virtually every turn, a valuable and friendly word of advice to Baylor's incoming freshmen would be offered, something to this effect: "Remember, this is college. High school may have come rather easily for you. This is different. It's going to be much more challenging and rigorous. You need to apply yourself and work hard. Here's your job description: *To be the best student you can possibly be.*" Sobering words.

We fully recognized, however, that students more frequently than not need a part-time job (including on-campus "work study" opportunities) to help pay their way through school. Also, extracurricular activities are important even for first-semester freshmen. We also wanted our newest Baylor Bears to become connected to and engaged in a local congregation. All that, taken together, is enormously time-consuming, if not overwhelming (at least in the early days of the daunting freshman year). Still and all, their basic "job" was to be a serious student employing their God-given talents to study and learn to the best of their ability.

The Parable of the Talents fits in perfectly with this mini-sermon about what incoming students face. We have talents; as a moral imperative, we must vigorously employ them.

We're to be energetically engaged and highly productive. Biblically expressed: "Faith without works is dead."

For these incoming freshmen, we allowed tips of the educational trade to flow their way. One basic point: Go to class. Studies have conclusively demonstrated that the most fundamental correlation between effort and academic success is literally going to class. We urged students to dismiss outright the notion or delusion that says, "Oh, she's so smart, she doesn't need to go to class. She just shows up for the final exam and hits it out of the park." In my years in and around colleges and law schools, never did I know that to be true.

The fable of the tortoise and the hare was more apropos. Steady as she goes, keep plowing ahead, and run the race put before you. Such shopworn nostrums convey a deep reality of student life: diligent effort, translated into careful reading and preparation and faithful class attendance, are the simple, common-sense ingredients of academic success.

This self-help regimen was augmented by the availability of tutoring and counseling services provided at the Paul Foster Success Center (named for the same Paul Foster who made the transformational gift to support the new campus home for Baylor's Business School).

It was very important for us to convey the how-tos during the earliest days of a student's college life. Creating good study habits, finding the optimal place to study (especially the library, including the iconic Armstrong-Browning Library, or in quiet and lovely spots of nature such as my favorite, the Garden of Contentment adjacent to ABL).

But before the instrumentalist focus on nuts and bolts, the Baylor Way was to introduce the incoming student body (including the almost five hundred transfer students who joined the Baylor family each year) to the great blessing and glory of the life of the mind.

"I think, therefore I am," said the ancients. "The unexamined life is not worth living," they continued. Thus, a grand tradition to convey the joyful seriousness of the academic enterprise was the very first official act of Welcome Week: Convocation, in full regalia, at the Ferrell Center. This formal procession, with the Baylor brass ensemble musically providing the attention-arresting focus of the entire freshman class, set the tone. The EVP-provost presided. Obligatory introductions and invocations, coupled with Scripture readings, added to the weighty nature of the proceedings.

The highlight was the keynote, delivered by a professor drawn from the thousand-strong community of teachers and scholars who comprise the Baylor faculty. Always inspiring, this address to the students was one of the high-water marks of the entire academic year. The collaborative joy of learning—and in particular the delight of opening up new chapters of intellectual interest—conveyed the theme of why we were gathering together. Integral to this homily was the inspiring goal of Christian higher education: to educate the whole person, not simply train someone for the job market.

Then, the denouement: the provost formally introduced the freshman class and asked that they be admitted to study at Baylor University as a class. Obviously, admission letters had long since gone out, acceptances dispatched, and deposits sent in. But those represented an individual act of the student in his separate capacity. Now, at Convocation, the entire class together was admitted to live and study at Baylor University. Sweet. The ceremony launched their educational journey on the path rightly called the Baylor Way.

Basic Questions

We gathered each autumn in a broader social and cultural context. American higher education was under searing scrutiny. Quite apart from issues of rising costs, graduation rates and job placement levels (so called "outcomes"), a twenty-first-century debate had emerged about first principles. What was college all about? What was the moral underpinning of the entire enterprise?

These existential questions—Who are we? Why are we here?—were the warp and woof of panel discussions at professional gatherings in higher education. We fretted together about these basic issues. The culture had dramatically shifted over the course of a generation, as we all witnessed daily in interactions with students—and especially with their fretful parents. Great issues were now largely neglected, if not ignored outright, even by the serious student (and vicariously, by his or her parents): How do I become a better person, more fully human? How can I best utilize my talents to serve others?

These lofty questions, grounded in admirable idealism (and in Christian values), were increasingly blunted and crowded out by the perceived exigencies of the age. In the global economy, with the voracious job-eating march of technology and ascendant economic theories grounded in values of increased efficiency, the issue of the twenty-first century turned instrumentalist: How does someone get a job after graduation?

Americans are practical. They look at the world around them through 20/20 lenses. They see jobs disappearing, companies merging and imposing efficiency-producing lay-offs, and jobs lost to overseas low-cost manufacturers. They see, politically, the emergence of populism throughout the Western world (as powerfully evidenced by the presidential election in 2016). Yet they also see vibrant entrepreneur-ship, and hard work and initiative handsomely rewarded, even as the eight-to-five predictability of more routine work at the factory or plant is relegated to the dustbin of history. These metatrends set a daunting task before faculty and administrators.

Happily, Baylor was part of a larger national conversation that got seriously underway early on in the twenty-first century. Baylor was blessed. By virtue of Vision 2012, controversial though it was, supplemented and extended by *Pro Futuris* (adopted unanimously by the Board of Regents in 2011), at Baylor we knew who we were. No identity crisis. Without being smug about it, we could say in effect, "Here we stand. We want to be a comprehensive research university that's unapologetically Christian. A tall order, sure. But we feel led to try. Indeed, in the non-Catholic world of higher education, we are—all modesty aside—the only show in town in view of our scale and size."

Throughout these conversations, echoes were heard throughout the corridors of American higher ed. Shots across the bow were fired by unlikely insurrectionists calling into question the pedagogical approaches of America's elite institutions. Harry Lewis, dean emeritus of Harvard College, wrote a haunting book about the hollowness of contemporary higher ed, especially in the ultra-elite Ivy League. The great questions of human existence were deliberately brushed aside. To wrestle with the fundamental questions of humanity was to make students—and faculty—

uncomfortable. How could we achieve consensus on such ethereal matters? Eat, drink, and be happy, for tomorrow we die.

In like manner, Tony Kronman, dean emeritus of the Yale Law School, authored a book lamenting that elite institutions had deliberately departed from the well-worn, admirable path of seeking wisdom. As with Dean Lewis, Dean Kronman yearned for a restoration of setting serious questions before suddenly emancipated teenagers entering their mature years, enjoying the exhilaration of freedom from the familial bonds of hearth and home, and suddenly empowered to strike out on a new course of self-identification and discovery.

So too, John Somerville, who devoted his entire teaching career to great public universities, penned a tome hauntingly entitled *The Decline of the Secular University*. Like Deans Lewis and Kronman, Professor Somerville's jeremiad scolded non-faith-based institutions for rendering themselves largely irrelevant to the fundamental issues of human existence.

In stark contrast stood Baylor—and the Baylor Way.

ON THE MOVE

The critique leveled by academic giants within the secular academy brought into bold relief the genius of Vision 2012—a hunger on the part of extraordinary professors of great accomplishment to be drawn to the lighthouse on the Brazos. As with *Field of Dreams*, "If you build it, they will come." The "it" being built wasn't a baseball diamond in a Midwestern cornfield, but something holy: a gathering place for eminent scholars and teachers who were committed to Baylor's Christian mission.

Over on the north side of University Parks, the mantra in the increasingly successful athletics program was "Victory with integrity." On the south side, on the historic but growing Waco campus, was an unstated slogan: "Academic excellence with Christian commitment."

Examples abound. One of my favorites comes from the humanities. As a C. S. Lewis aficionado, I glom onto books (or at least book reviews, when reading time fails) about the great man. As a dad, I loved reading *The Chronicles of Narnia* aloud to our children. With them, I wept when Aslan met his earthly doom at the hands of the White Witch. Call it a lifelong commitment to learning more about this one-time atheist who came to faith. Having devoured a fabulous book about the Cambridge-Oxford don entitled *The Narnian*, I was overjoyed to learn that the author, renowned Wheaton College professor Alan Jacobs, would be in residence at Baylor for a semester. Although my role in recruiting Alan (as so frequently was the case) was virtually nil, sure enough, the semester in residence sealed the hoped-for deal. Alan moved from his beloved (and greatly admired) perch at Wheaton to Baylor.

Not long after Alan had taken up full-time residence in Waco, I found myself on a panel under the impressive auspices of Baylor's Institute of Faith and Learning (headed by theologically trained Darin Davis), yet another shoot flowering from the Vision 2012 branch. The conference theme was "Educating for Wisdom in the 21st Century." The topic itself suggested the nature and thrust of what twenty-first-century Baylor was seeking to foster; as might reasonably have been predicted, fellow academics and administrators poured into Waco from around the country to participate, listen, and learn. Among the panel participants was the deeply impressive president of Wheaton, Phil Ryken. A bit shamefaced, I mumbled a quasi-apology to Phil for having "poached" Alan Jacobs from his long-settled academic home on the outskirts of Chicago. Phil was immediately reassuring: "Ken, not to worry. This is good for Alan. He now has people to talk to."

Scope and scale. Baylor's sheer size and comprehensiveness created a larger, highly energetic community of scholars and teachers. America's religiously affiliated colleges and universities are precious, and many may eagerly want to grow and expand, and God bless them if they can and do. Baylor, however, had an enormous head start, especially with the pro-growth attitudes of key leaders and governing boards along the almost two-century institutional journey.

Appropriate for Texas, the Baylor ethos was "Let's get it done" and "Why not?" Our Vision 2012—and now *Pro Futuris*—embraced expansion. "Let's grow the enterprise" carried the day.

In the sciences (and, more generally, STEM—science, technology, engineering and mathematics), the prevailing attitude in Vision 2012 and *Pro Futuris* was "Let's improve, let's pursue excellence." Taking a page from Jim Collins's concept of going from "good to great," Baylor's academic flywheel was turning faster and faster. Excellence begets excellence.

The key player in the important institutional move to higher research was a brilliant physicist, Truell Hyde, one of several extraordinarily able vice provosts. Truell was, in a word, invaluable in the university's march toward high research status.

Consider chemistry. Pat Farmer, a committed believer, was wooed away from UC-Irvine, where he'd amassed a superb record in teaching and research. A move from Southern California to Texas has many advantages, but climate is not among them. But to Baylor Pat Farmer came, to serve as chair of the Chemistry Department. Soon, Pat recruited John Wood, previously tenured at Yale and recently returned to his native Colorado. Both Pat and John were drawn to Baylor because of our now-settled ambition of being a top-tier research university firmly committed to a Christian worldview.

So too, Dennis O'Neal moved upriver from his beloved Texas A&M, where he'd served as chair of mechanical engineering (one of many A&M academic strengths) to take on the mantle as dean of Baylor's burgeoning School of Engineering and Computer Science. Twentieth-century Baylor had matured into the era of the knowledge economy, with a strong policy commitment to continued growth in STEM. Following in Dean O'Neal's path was renowned biologist Richard Romo, and from Pat Farmer's Southland, a UCLA-chaired professor, Dwayne Simmons.

To be sure, Baylor will never be M.I.T. or Cal Tech, nor should it try. It can, however, achieve excellence in research that promotes human flourishing. Marlan Scully, chaired at both Princeton and Texas A&M, opened a major quantum physics research lab at Baylor, illustrating the reality that, like Aslan in the Chronicles of Narnia, Baylor is "on the move."

Not to overlook the happy fact that Baylor is already "best in class" in arenas that go to the heart of the Christian mission. I previously mentioned Byron Johnson, a renowned sociologist and criminologist who left the charms of Philadelphia and the University of Pennsylvania to launch the Institute for the Studies of Religion. ISR has become a gathering place for renowned sociologists who set the standard for superb research with enormous influence on public policy and the broader culture. Byron's path-breaking book, *More God, Less Crime*, empirically demonstrates the connection between Christian belief and radical transformation of broken lives.

His codirector at ISR, Rodney Stark, produces one bestseller after another, including my favorite, *The Triumph of Christianity*. (Early on in my tenure at Pat Neff Hall, I ran into Rodney in the hallway and lavished praise on his earlier book, *The Rise of Christianity*. With a harrumph, Rodney was dismissive. "That's a very bad book," he growled. "Read this one instead." To my great benefit, I added *The Triumph of Christianity* to my reading list.)

Baylor's academic hall of fame, figuratively speaking, is already impressive and is happily ever-growing. It rivals Cooperstown in length and breadth—and of course, is older than America's pastime itself.

Final example: Richard Rankin Russell, who came to Baylor early on after completing his doctoral work in English at the University of North Carolina in Chapel Hill. Embodying his research done primarily under the gentle umbrella of Baylor's Department of English, Richard's magnum opus, *Seamus Heaney's Regions*, won the internationally prestigious Warren-Brooks Award for Outstanding Literary Criticism in 2015.

"Beauty is truth, and truth beauty," said the romantics. At Baylor, scholars such as Richard Rankin Russell, Byron Johnson, Alan Jacobs, Pat Farmer, Richard Romo, Marlan Scully, and many others productively labor in their various vineyards creating beauty and discovering truth.

The apostle Paul guided his readers in the early church

"to think on these things"—with *excellence* at the center of that concentrated focus of thought. That, in a word, is twenty-first-century Baylor academics. In both science (STEM) and the humanities, these luminaries helped fashion the twenty-first-century version of the Baylor Way.

8

INCLUSION

GOOD THINGS HAPPEN IN SUNDAY SCHOOL. ONE IS THE TRANSMIT-
ting of inspiring, uplifting songs down through the generations. One children's song of enduring moral power and
continuing currency, especially in light of cultural trends in
America—and indeed in much of the Western world—is a
sweet song of inclusion: "Red and yellow, black and white,
they are precious in his sight; Jesus loves the little children
of the world." The song complements the warmly familiar
refrain: "Jesus loves me, this I know."

Combining the inspiring Gospel portrayal of Christ
welcoming little children into his loving arms (against his
disciples' snarly objections) with the parable of the Good
Samaritan creates a powerful theological perspective
informing a Christian worldview: every person, without
exception, is of eternal value. The apostle Paul likewise
trumpeted the unifying concept of universal inclusion in
the Kingdom. In Christian thinking, there's no American
or Russian, but all are "one in Christ Jesus."

In a broken world, this message of "Welcome" rather
than "You're an outsider" has enormous appeal. The
universality-vision also spawns efforts to tear down walls
and to build bridges. Little wonder that the greatest social
reforms over the last two centuries—from abolitionism in

the nineteenth century to the civil rights movement in the twentieth—emerged out of decidedly Christian circles.

DEMANDS

The secular version of this Christian theme of universality and inclusion travels under the familiar label of "diversity." American higher education has been at the forefront of what has now become a cultural battleground. Vigorous debates over inclusivity and the lack thereof—especially ethnic and racial diversity—erupted across American campuses in the fall of 2015 and spring of 2016.

A flash point was the University of Missouri at Columbia. With geographic proximity to Ferguson, Missouri, where a deadly police shooting inflamed large segments of the African-American community and captured the nation's attention for days on end, Mizzou experienced a period of student-generated unrest quickly leading to the ouster (by resignation) of the flagship campus's president. The end came when the Tigers football team—vocally supported by the head coach—threatened to go on strike and boycott an upcoming game unless campus leadership changed.

College football programs wield enormous power, especially with alumni and donors. The unenviable choice was either football or presidential continuity. In short order, the president resigned. At Mizzou, football reigned supreme.

Similar dramas played out across the country. Presidents' offices were occupied, student demands were pressed, and routine campus life significantly disrupted. Not since the antiwar demonstrations of the sixties had higher education been so engulfed in boiling social controversy.

Out of the campus cauldron emerged yet another

issue—the demand for renaming iconic campus buildings and programs. Headlines blazed through the daily press, recounting demands at Yale to rename Calhoun College (in view of the slaveholding of the antebellum senator from South Carolina) and at Princeton to jettison the name of the fabled Woodrow Wilson School. Princeton's president—and future U.S. president—was wedded to the execrable practice of segregation.

Naming issues aside, what gave practical unity to the pro-diversity ferment was a series of "demands." High on the list was the creation of a dedicated office focusing on increasing diversity, especially racial and ethnic diversity among faculty and the student body. Aided by ubiquitous networking through social media, the demands pressed by student leaders (frequently supported by faculty) embodied a highly consistent framework across American campuses. And the demands were usually met with favor. One Ivy League president committed $50 million to the overall effort to expand and deepen inclusion.

COMPELLING INTERESTS

The superbly organized effort to change the face of American higher education unfolded against the backdrop of a long-running and deeply divisive legal debate over line-drawing on the basis of race or other immutable characteristics. In service of a fairer, more representative student body, public university officials had fashioned various approaches to admissions. Early on, the University of California created a regime of actual set-asides for medical school slots. Under the Golden State's approach, x number of slots in medical school would be formally reserved for students of color. That set-aside or "quota" system spawned a constitutional challenge by a white candidate, Allan Bakke, who was denied admission—notwithstanding his sterling credentials.

In a watershed decision, the U.S. Supreme Court said no to the California authorities. A set-aside or quota system was constitutionally unacceptable. However, in a controlling opinion in the deeply divided tribunal, Justice Lewis Powell Jr. articulated what was seen as a middle course. Quotas or set-asides went too far, and were deemed to violate the Fourteenth Amendment's demand of equality under the law (the concept of "equal protection"). At the same time, the Solomonic middle ground was to permit colleges and universities to consider race as part of the larger, holistic bundle of considerations assessed in the admissions process. In Justice Powell's formulation, race could serve as a "compelling" interest to be taken into account along with the other elements of admissions criteria. But that interest would have to be served by careful framing—or, in the court's jargon, "narrowly tailored" to serve the state's "compelling" interest.

In the wake of the Bakke case, a generation-long constitutional battle unfolded. Some programs—such as that of the University of Michigan Law School—were upheld. As the Supreme Court saw it, the Ann Arbor sages had kept the balance true. They had considered race, but only as part of the bigger picture. "Holistic" evaluation was deemed the key to passing constitutional muster. Other regimes, including the University of Texas's undergrad admissions program, were struck down as too rigidly employing race or ethnicity as a decisive criterion. The issue was, at best, murky, and college leaders kept seeking greater clarity from the nation's highest court. What was permissible? What fell short of the constitutional standard?

In a recent treatment of the issue, the Supreme Court sustained UT's race-conscious admissions program as having steered safely through the course charted decades earlier by Justice Powell in the California case. Race or ethnicity was a factor, but only one among many that could be properly taken into account. Authored by the key centrist on the court, Justice Anthony Kennedy (appointed by President Reagan), the decision (known as the Fisher case) at long last pointed the way for public colleges and universities to follow.

PUBLIC AND PRIVATE

The Constitution, of course, applies to governmental action. Baylor is unconstrained by the Constitution, the Bill of Rights, and the other seventeen Amendments, since it's a private entity chartered under state law (and indeed, chartered by the Republic of Texas prior to statehood). But that limitation is more theoretical than real. In the post-World War II era, and particularly during the presidency of Texas's own Lyndon Johnson, various federal programs were created to benefit education at all levels. With federal largesse come federal constraints. As a practical matter, under Department of Education regulations, as well as congressional enactments, private institutions are in effect on a legal par with public institutions created and supported by governmental action.

The exceptions are the bold institutions that set their faces against federal aid. Grove City College in Pennsylvania and Hillsdale College in Michigan, two highly respected, academically rigorous liberal arts institutions with long, proud histories, spurn any and all forms of federal aid. For many private institutions which don't seek federally funded research grants, the long arm of federal regulation reaches them by virtue of the student financial aid programs, such as Pell grants. Since over 90 percent of Baylor students receive some form of financial aid, including university-provided scholarships, the federal-regulatory trigger captures virtually all institutions of higher education in the country. With federal aid, including Pell grants, come the strings of regulatory control.

The constitutional and legal issues thus confront private colleges and universities in essentially the same manner as the great public institutions, such as the University of California and the University of Texas, that gave rise to the epic constitutional struggles over affirmative action.

FOR DIVERSITY AT BAYLOR

Baylor's story has, thus far, avoided the calumny and rancor that swept over American campuses in 2015–2016. No buildings were occupied, no threats of student-inspired strikes were issued. To the contrary, throughout the 2015–2016 academic year, the campus engaged in a vigorous conversation about inclusion.

Early fall brought about a provost-appointed committee, which focused narrowly on the issue of a new position dedicated to diversity and inclusion. How do we get a Chief Diversity Officer, and what would that model look like? The process featured a series of "town hall" meetings among faculty (students and staff weren't included).

The Baylor Way is to seek to avoid conflict. But strong statements were made as the debate unfolded. Feelings were hurt. The faculty—again, over a thousand strong—found themselves dividing into competing camps. Assiduously avoiding labels, I viewed my suddenly warring colleagues as genuine and sincere, divided by honest differences of opinion. In one community, the very modest numbers of women and minority professors cried out for stronger, more focused efforts to achieve greater inclusion. The Chief Diversity Officer mechanism was, under this view, a readily available, commonly employed way to achieve that goal. On the other side, deep-seated concerns were expressed about compromising standards of excellence, and in particular the creation of what was feared to be a new layer of potentially meddlesome university bureaucracy. Above all, the battle lines were drawn specifically over the creation of an office that was dedicated to enhancing and expanding diversity.

A basic maxim from constitutional law helped provide the biblical "balm in Gilead." The answer to speech with which you disagree is…more speech. And thus in the spring of 2016, the campus-wide conversation was expanded. Led by the extraordinary Professor Lori Baker, whose magnificent work (as we previously described) on the U.S. border in identifying the remains of immigrants perilously crossing into the land of liberty and opportunity had gained national acclaim, a presidential committee—consisting not only of faculty, but students and staff as well—embarked on a more thorough, open-ended examination of the laudable goal of enhancing inclusion without embracing from the start a particular means to that universally shared end. Creating that mechanism proved beneficial, as the spring semester unfolded in a civil campus-wide conversation more congruent with the Baylor Way. In short, the conversation about diversity became more inclusive of the broader campus community.

So too, the discussions with student groups proceeded

in a civil, professional manner. No demonstrations marred the blessed peace that prevails day to day on the beautiful Baylor campus.

With the guidance of Kevin Jackson, vice president for student life, the leaders of student groups of color presented recommendations and suggestions—not demands. That seemingly innocuous difference in formulation made all the difference in the world. Unions make "demands" on management. Kidnappers make "demands" on the hapless families of victims. The word itself connotes conflict rooted in an adversarial relationship.

That was not the Baylor Way. The unifying Christian worldview counseled in favor of a different approach.

"Come let us reason together" provided the moral scaffolding to undergird and support a lively conversation among people of good will who harbored honest differences of opinion—a genuine conflict of visions. Christian higher education, as embodied in Vision 2012 and *Pro Futuris*, lifted up Saint Francis-inspired goals: "Lord, make me an instrument of thy peace."

That was—and is—the Baylor Way.

9

EXPLOSION

MOVE-IN DAY WAS COMPLETE, WELCOME WEEK HAD GONE SWIM-mingly, and the new academic year—2015–2016—loomed just ahead, filled with promise.

Then came the explosion. A closely watched rape trial was underway at the McLennan County Courthouse, a magnificent structure symbolizing the community-unifying goal of justice for all. Sam Ukwuachu, a supertalented defensive end on Baylor's football team who'd transferred from football powerhouse Boise State, was in the dock, charged with an egregious offense against basic human dignity. Sam's rape trial launched a crisis. Suddenly, for all the wrong reasons, Baylor football was thrust into the national limelight.

THE BACKGROUND

Triggering this unexpected explosion was a provocative online piece by the wildly popular homegrown periodical, *Texas Monthly*. Based in Austin, and unremittingly progressive in tone, TM published a harshly critical online piece just as preseason was drawing to a close, claiming that, in effect, a rape culture had grown up in the fabulously successful football program under the turbo-charged leadership of Coach Art Briles. This was the first anyone around the

Executive Council round table had heard anything of the sort.

A terrible pall fell over the conference room in Pat Neff 100. Just hours before, we'd all been exulting in the excitement of a new year. Football was an integral part of what would soon unfold that autumn. After all, in a few short years, Coach Briles had built a national powerhouse on the banks of the Brazos. And his dream of an on-campus stadium had come true. The house that RG III built was, in fact, the house built by Art Briles and Drayton McLane Jr.; Coach Briles was the inspiration, and Drayton—the dreamer of great dreams—was the driving force.

Coach and Drayton were joined by a cracker-jack in-house development team, augmented by members of the Board of Regents, especially former chairman Dary Stone. The staff and regent volunteers poured themselves into the unprecedented fundraising effort. They had triumphed. And year one at McLane had gone beautifully, marred only by injuries to two key quarterbacks. Even then, the 2015 season had ended with a record-shattering offensive display in Orlando as the Baylor Bears overwhelmed the Tar Heels of North Carolina with a high-speed "wildcat" offense (no quarterback).

For his part, Coach Briles had quickly built an eye-popping football program that matched the stunningly impressive stadium, which in short order became a gathering place for the broader community, not just the Baylor family. Indeed, at Coach Briles's urging, the very first game played at McLane Stadium was not a Baylor Bears high-octane display of razzle-dazzle offense, but a high school match-up straight out of *Friday Night Lights*. Baylor was making a statement: McLane Stadium is for all of us, not just for Baylor Nation on college game day.

McLane Stadium—which got its name just prior to opening, with Coach Briles insisting that it carry the McLane family name rather than the institutionalized, plain-vanilla "Baylor Stadium"—brought tens of thousands of fans and friends to the banks of the Brazos. Season ticket sales skyrocketed. Games were now sold out. At the aging Floyd Casey Stadium, albeit home to great memories over a half century, we worked hard to fill the seats. The occasional sell-out would occur when, say, the Longhorns came to Waco and eagerly bought up the thousands of unwanted tickets. That was then. Now, ESPN brought "Game Day" to campus, and the prevailing colors were the beautiful gold of the Baylor Line and shades of Baylor green sprinkled in. The optics were even better than at green-and-gold-dominated Lambeau Field in Green Bay.

And so Sam Ukwuachu came. He'd traveled north from Houston, where he'd done well enough academically in high school while his strength and speed attracted attention from gridiron programs across the country. He chose national powerhouse Boise State, but he was soon unhappy and homesick. His head football coach looked after him, thought he should be closer to home, called Coach Briles, and soon Sam was a Baylor Bear, although he never played football at Baylor.

When Sam was charged with the unspeakably horrible act of rape, he protested his innocence and defended himself vigorously. Devastating testimony by a former girlfriend from Boise State—who contradicted Sam's testimony of nonviolence—likely sealed his fate.

The McLennan County jury found him guilty, but fashioned an oddly lenient sentence—probation. As I write, Sam continues to protest his innocence, and to seek redress in the courts. But the jury verdict stands, and Sam is thus a convicted felon.

BAYLOR RESPONDS

Even in the best of college athletic programs, horrible deeds are done. We're a fallen race. The nationally debated case of the Stanford swimmer, convicted of rape but given a lenient sentence, once again brought into sharp focus the problem of interpersonal violence on and around college campuses, and in particular, sexual assault. National statistics were frequently reported to the effect that one in five young women are sexually assaulted (or are otherwise victims of interpersonal violence) during their college years. Sam's case provided the jumping off point for *Texas Monthly*'s provocative thesis that with all of its vaunted success, Coach Briles's program was infected by a culture of violence against women.

We rolled into action. A crisis management team was set up, the Board of Regents was promptly informed (first through the leadership), and an initial recommendation was made. Specifically, I commissioned Baylor's faculty athletic representative (a post required under NCAA procedures) to conduct an internal inquiry into the charges. By design, this faculty representative operates outside of and independent of the Athletic Department. Serving in a watchdog capacity as a form of check and balance, the faculty representative reports directly to the president.

Jeremy Counseller, a respected law professor, took on the role. Within several days, he reported back in a one-page summary that contained only the background of his appointment, plus his solitary recommendation—that an outside investigation should be conducted. That is, no one inside or connected to the university should be retained to provide a truly independent, honest assessment of the situation.

So it was that Pepper Hamilton, a respected Philadelphia law firm, was retained. Their work began in early September 2015 and concluded in May 2016. To assure the independence of its work, the Pepper Hamilton lawyers reported directly to a special three-person committee of Baylor's Board of Regents. That structure remained in place throughout the lengthy process, culminating in a verbal presentation—with numerous PowerPoint slides—to the board in mid-May 2016.

The final product was twofold: a set of "findings of fact," reported by the Board of Regents, and a lengthy set of recommendations from the law firm. There was no "report" in the traditional sense. The board's findings and Pepper Hamilton's recommendations were publicly released, leading to events that I describe in the next chapter.

The findings were deeply troubling. Moral outrage was the order of the day throughout the country. This was page one, above-the-fold news. Searing criticism unfolded, not simply of the football program but of Baylor overall. The university's response to interpersonal violence (including sexual assault) was found wanting. The criticisms were directed at what I call "first responders," including campus law enforcement, health services, and counseling. Pepper Hamilton's findings were summarized as a "fundamental failure" on the part of the university. This quickly became the prevailing narrative, one that was reinforced as additional victims (some of whom had graduated) came forward to reveal their tragic experiences. These were chronicled in dramatic ways by ESPN's hard-hitting program "Outside the Lines."

Baylor—not just the football program—became a pariah.

Victims' stories moved the thoughtful observer or listener to a powerful combination of empathy and outrage. One's heart goes out to the victim; a second later, waves of outrage wash over the empathetic observer. How could this have happened? Who fell asleep at the switch? Who failed to protect these young women, and why? Did coaches turn a blind eye to reports of unconscionable acts by superstar players—or even nonsuperstars—who abused young women? Did "first responders" on the university's payroll turn a deaf ear to distraught complaints of sexual violence, including rape? How could this be, especially at a self-professed Christian university?

I made it clear that as chief executive, I accepted responsibility for any shortcomings or failings on the university's part. No act of sexual violence can be tolerated, period, even off campus (which is where all the serious incidents, as reported, took place). And no one, regardless of how important the student-athlete was to program success, was to be above the law. Basic decency, reinforced by the Christian commitment to creating a caring community, called for the gold standard with respect to prevention in the first place, and effective response if prevention safeguards failed.

THE OTHER SIDE

As the old saying goes, there are usually two sides to the story. Pepper Hamilton's recommendations, coupled with the Board of Regents' "findings of fact," created a toxic killer of a narrative. The devastating conclusion—a fundamental failure of the institution itself—echoed throughout campus and demoralized Baylor Nation. An operational failure of the highest order had been identified, with profound impacts on victims and their families.

The other side of the story was left untold. Campus safety—and the safety of our students in all respects, including freedom from interpersonal violence—was a high priority throughout my years of servant-leadership. The idea that Pat Neff Hall was oblivious to student safety concerns was belied not only by common sense and basic human decency, but refuted by the facts.

Here, in brief, is the other side of the story.

In the fall of 2010, the Executive Committee round table focused specifically on issues of student safety arising out of an investigation by the Department of Education's Office of Civil Rights (OCR) into a tragic student death at Eastern Michigan University. The twenty-two-year-old student was found dead in her residence hall after having been sexually assaulted and brutally beaten. The government's devastating report was issued in November 2010. Baylor's Executive Committee promptly determined to establish a Baylor Student Safety Concern Task Force to examine all issues relating to student safety, including but by no means limited to interpersonal violence.

This task force had an outstanding group of members. In January 2011, five student leaders, including Student Body President Michael Wright, joined with Police Chief Jim Doak and Executive Committee member Kevin Jackson (vice president for student life), plus other key staff members, to begin their work early in the new semester. The task force held on-campus hearings. Broad participation was invited.

In the meantime, additional voices were raised across the nation. As the Baylor task force was operating at full speed, sixteen Yale students filed a complaint with respect to the prevailing campus climate there. One particularly disturbing incident included a ribald Yale fraternity chant: "No means yes." The brothers' outrageous chant then went a perverse step further in descending into the realm of raucous indignity.

In April 2011, OCR published its first "Dear Colleague" letter with respect to responsibilities under Title IX. In contrast to a common misunderstanding, the letter did not embody or reflect law. It wasn't law in any sense of the word. It wasn't reporting an act of Congress, nor was it setting forth an administrative regulation enjoying the force of law. It was a letter providing guidance, not the direction that law enjoys. Nor did that guidance call for the appointment of a full-time Title IX coordinator. To the contrary, that administrative step from the government was more than three years away.

Three days after OCR's "Dear Colleague" letter appeared, a public panel discussion took place on the Baylor campus. I joined Vice President Jackson and Student Body President Wright in discussing a wide range of student safety issues, and took questions from the floor. This on-campus conversation was illustrative of what was underway around the nation. Everyone was aware of myriad concerns about student safety, including freedom from interpersonal violence. No one in Pat Neff Hall had his or her head in the sand, nor averted his or her gaze to avoid facing unpleasantness—or worse.

The work of the campus task force was completed, and in the fall of 2012, a Campus Safety Committee was formed. This committee pulled together stakeholders from all across campus to discuss any and all threats to student safety. Issues relating to sexual assault were an integral part of the broad mandate the committee examined.

For its first three years, the Campus Safety Committee was chaired by Vice President Jackson. Its work enjoyed the unalloyed support of the entire Executive Council. Then in June 2013, I issued a memorandum creating a specialized Task Force Review of Sexual Violence to conduct a comprehensive review of Baylor's policies and practices relating to sexual violence. This task force (operating at the same time as the Campus Safety Committee) was formed in response to the recommendations and concerns expressed by John Whelan, our head of human resources.

Action items quickly emerged. The entering freshman class in August of 2013 was specifically briefed by a senior Student Life staff member on what was expected in terms of proper, upright behavior. Entering students were provided with a copy of OCR's "Know Your Rights" summary, along with a highly specific cover letter from Vice President Jackson. The following month (September 2013), the "Do Something!" campaign was launched—a sexual assault prevention campaign hosted the week after Labor Day. The campaign was sponsored by Baylor's Sexual Assault Advisory Board chaired by Dr. Cheryl Wooten, an outstanding leader recognized across the nation for her expertise in dealing with the horror and trauma of sexual violence.

The story continues with the appointment of an Executive Committee member, Dr. Karla Leeper, as the Title IX coordinator, to succeed the departing John Whelan, our head of human resources who left to return to Indiana as head of HR at IU-Bloomington. This basic fact stands uncontested—at no time did Baylor University fail to have a high-level Title IX coordinator in place. Never. Not for one instant.

The suggestion that the administration somehow failed to have a Title IX coordinator in compliance with OCR guidance is demonstrably wrong. Indeed, Baylor was months ahead of OCR's later guidance that the issues swirling around Title IX were sufficiently complex that a full-time coordinator was called for. Baylor was way ahead of the curve.

Following numerous meetings of the specialized task force, the administration engaged a leading consulting firm, Margolis Healy & Associates, to assess Baylor's compliance with Title IX and the Clery Act (a federal law requiring reports of on-campus assaults; note the key requirement of "on-campus"). Within a few short months, Margolis Healy recommended the appointment of a full-time Title IX coordinator. At the round table, the Executive Committee discussed that recommendation, along with others (including our shortcomings in reporting under the Clery Act). Without dissent, the committee embraced the consulting firm's recommendation, and by October 2014, Patty Crawford was in place in her full-time role.

In the meantime, the Sexual Assault Advisory Board developed an elaborate prevention proposal to launch in the fall of 2014. That exemplary proposal resulted in the "Bear Up Now" program, designed to prevent all forms of interpersonal violence. In August and September 2014, a full year before the *Texas Monthly* neutron-bomb report, widespread campus training for all students was launched. In particular, the effort featured the renowned Green Dot program (developed by the federal government in response to sexual violence reports at the Air Force Academy). Green Dot is a state-of-the-art program that sets the standard for the pivotally important function of bystander intervention.

Throughout late August 2014, almost 150 peer-leader educators at Baylor were trained in prevention; those peer leaders then led elaborate prevention education sessions in small groups with community leaders and their residents. Beloved Baylor Police Officer Kandy Knowles guided numerous discussions with students in residence hall meetings early on in the new academic year.

Chapel, the cherished Baylor tradition, featured the highly impressive Rachel Sibley and others in the Baylor community who were outspoken on the subject of preventing sexual violence. The faculty and staff likewise joined in the effort. Over a three-month period from August through October 2014, almost two thousand faculty, staff, and student workers completed training sessions on both Title IX and the Violence Against Women Act, a measure which had been signed into law (a reauthorization) by President Obama in the early spring of 2013.

Baylor loves its students. I love the students. We want them not only to be safe, but to flourish. We worked hard to achieve that goal in a fallen world, where all too often students will yield to temptations all around them.

We could always do more. And the silver lining of the nine-month ordeal culminating in the events of May 2016 is that no university is more focused on Title IX-related prevention and effective response than our beloved Baylor.

To be sure, there were failures and shortcomings. In particular, I lament the now-known fact that first responders were, at best, insensitive to reports of sexual violence. But

I didn't know. I had an open door policy at Pat Neff for students, faculty, staff, and regents. Had I known what is now being reported, the administration would have taken decisive action.

As I write, the facts as to individual cases are being ping-ponged about by numerous parties in multiple pending lawsuits. Some day we may know the truth. I desire and await the truth, along with so many others in Baylor Nation and beyond.

I advocated transparency from the very start of the investigation, as I was the one ultimately accountable. These former colleagues worked for me. The buck stops here.

10

FAREWELL

SPRING GRADUATION 2016 WAS A JOY. AS TRADITION HOLDS, I greeted and hugged every Baylor graduate who walked (or otherwise traversed) the Ferrell Center stage. The Pepper Hamilton report seemed to fade into the background. We were still standing, and the mood seemed upbeat. The spirit at Baylor graduation was joyful as always. We sang the sweet songs of Baylor commencement ceremonies: "God Bless America" and "Great Is Thy Faithfulness." And, of course, we closed with "That Good Old Baylor Line." Almost three thousand graduates—both undergrads and graduate students—received their diplomas in ceremonies over the course of Friday afternoon and Saturday morning and afternoon. Then, after an early church service on Sunday morning, I headed down to San Marcos, south of Austin, to speak at the San Marcos Academy graduation. The high school graduates—a handful heading for Baylor—were from literally all over the world, especially China. This was America at its welcoming best.

Then, bidding farewell to my San Marcos friends, off I went to Atlanta for a meeting, and then quickly back to campus again. It was the Tuesday after graduation weekend—only three days had passed since the three uplifting ceremonies at the Ferrell Center. All seemed peaceful.

The news came abruptly. The thunderbolt was delivered by the university's lawyer, Ray Cotton, a renowned D.C. practitioner. I was being fired as president. I'd run out of bullets, I was informed.

A very able attorney whom I'd come to know well, Ray Cotton had been kind and thoughtful to me over the years, but at day's end, he was the lawyer for the university, which is—and rightly so—controlled by the Board of Regents. The regents had decided. I was told that their decision was unanimous (I was later told in confidence by a Baylor regent that the vote had not in fact been unanimous). That came as a complete shock, a punch in the gut. But I accepted it. Gladly would I serve, and so cheerfully I must accept the regents' death sentence.

It was May 16. I was to step aside as president on either June 1 or July 1. Terms and conditions on my continued service as chancellor would be discussed in short order.

In announcing my firing, I was also to take several steps, including accepting responsibility for the various events—and shortcomings—reported to the board by Pepper Hamilton. In addition, I was to announce that Executive Council member Reagan Ramsower was becoming executive vice president—the clear number two officer in the university—and that L. Gregory Jones, our new executive vice president and provost, would simply serve hereafter as provost.

The news was stunning and yet not entirely unexpected. Quietly, I'd been living on borrowed time.

For nearly five years, the board's leadership had worked to ease me out of the CEO role and slot me instead into the nonexecutive position of chancellor, primarily a fundraiser. For various reasons, I wasn't satisfying the board's vision of a CEO. In their view, I was instead to be an outside person building the university through raising money. Although I relished the fundraising task, I'd resisted the dramatic change in roles. No longer would I be placing my imprint, however modest, on the university. Yet, as I saw it, I could energetically continue to fundraise through the daily work of the presidency.

Indeed, through the able leadership of Dave Rosselli, who we'd enticed to join the Baylor family from the University of Southern California, we were well on our way in laying the groundwork for a major capital campaign. Dave and I had traveled to and fro—including to California and Arizona in recent weeks—to prepare for that eagerly anticipated (and much-needed) capital campaign.

But the regents' response to the Pepper Hamilton "report" had laid me low. I was out as president, and not of my own volition. I would remain as chancellor, as well as a tenured faculty member at the Baylor Law School. Coach Art Briles was also out, as was the highly lauded Athletic Director Ian McCaw. Likewise, two Athletics Department staff members, Colin Shillinglaw and the universally admired and beloved Tom Hill, would be terminated. (The circumstances in each instance varied, but the end result was the conclusion of their service to the university.)

The irony was palpable. On three separate occasions over my six years of service, I'd determined that the right course of action was to resign from the presidency and simply carry on my role as a member of the Baylor Law School faculty. I loved the law school, and relished teaching my course in current constitutional issues. The law school was, in a sense, my home base. If I could simply cross over University Parks Drive from the main campus and settle into the comfortable confines of that gorgeous building beautifully situated on the banks of the Brazos, with its extraordinary dean and exemplary faculty, I'd be safe.

But my safety zone was soon gone. I would be in exile.

The background story briefly told is this: in October 2011, I threatened to resign from the presidency (two years before my appointment as president and chancellor) by virtue of what I considered unacceptably inappropriate conduct—and comments—by the board's chairman, Buddy Jones.

The university's long-running feud with the Baylor Alumni Association had erupted during homecoming celebrations in 2011. On an October afternoon at Floyd Casey Stadium, at halftime, the Baylor Alumni Association had—consistent with tradition—bestowed its annual set of honors on various BAA-endorsed luminaries. Joy Reynolds, widow of legendary Baylor president Dr. Herbert Reynolds, went onto the field, escorted by her son, Kent. This venerable figure in Baylor life was to present the awards. The public announcements then followed, with the awards duly presented. The BAA had entered center stage at the single most university-honoring event of the year.

The chairman of the Baylor Board of Regents was displeased. In strong language, both in person and in writing, he expressed profound displeasure with the university for having permitted its platform to be used by the BAA to carry on its unwelcome mission. Chairman Jones's disapprobation was severe, and it was strongly expressed.

For months, I'd been laboring day after day to bring the BAA in-house, and had pursued—if unsuccessfully— the announced policy of courtesy, respect, and hospitality toward the BAA. I'd restated that policy again and again.

Here, however, was a clear instance of the Board of Regents' leadership seeking to overrule the administration. I thought that entirely improper. I made it clear, emphatically so, that I couldn't continue to serve as president as a matter of principle. In short, I would return to teaching law (and perhaps resuming the part-time practice I'd agreed to leave upon becoming president).

A leader of the regents telephoned me and talked me off the ledge. "You may be the only person who can lead us," he said. He assured me that the leadership situation was under control. I relented and went back to work. At the next game, that same leader gave me a kiss on the cheek. The crisis had passed.

The second episode occurred in April 2012. Chairman Jones was leaving the chairmanship, and indeed completing his nine years of service (three terms of three years each). I was summoned to meet with him and another regent at the chairman's powerhouse lobbying office in Austin for my year-end review. It went well. The review—as with literally every one of my year-end reviews—was highly laudatory. The university was doing well, indeed thriving. We were building Baylor. "Keep up the good work," was the message. A generous bonus provided tangible proof that the year (academic year 2011–2012) had gone well. (That, of course, was the year of RG III's Heisman and the women's basketball team's national championship.)

But an additional point was soon made. To improve execution within the administration, a new organizational chart was to be implemented. It was simply presented to me, a fait accompli. The structure of the Executive Committee's round table would be modified; rather than a clear number two officer in the person of the Executive Vice President and Provost (Elizabeth Davis), there would now be three senior officers reporting to the president/CEO. The other vice presidents would remain in their respective positions, reporting not to the president but to one of the respective senior officers. The culture of the round table—all voices equal, including my own—was to shift.

Wisely or no, I acquiesced. For long months, I'd resisted the Board of Regents' continuing calls to have a clearly designated chief operating officer other than the provost. To my mind, the COO was Elizabeth Davis, our EVP and provost. I hadn't formulated that title; to the contrary, the title was longstanding and reflected an administrative arrangement that made perfect sense for Baylor—and indeed for higher education more generally. (I'd cross-checked this with, among others, Condoleezza Rice, who'd served as both provost and COO of Stanford.) In my view, the university's chief academic officer should in fact be the number two person in the administrative structure. The board's new structure, in practical effect, created three senior officers of equal rank. It was, functionally, a demotion of the EVP-provost and an elevation of two others—the CFO and the head of development (who was also given responsibility for strategic initiatives).

This was a classic trade-off. No outside COO would be imposed on what I considered a healthy, open, and collaborative structure. That was good. At the same time, several of my colleagues were organizationally demoted. They would now report to senior vice presidents.

I brought back the news to campus. It was not well received. The effect around the round table was predictable. Like George Orwell's *Animal Farm*, some colleagues were "more equal" than others. I'd failed to fight for an important principle: the collaborative culture of the Executive Council.

The most dramatic episode occurred in the summer and fall of 2013. It followed on the heels of several months of gentle nudging back in 2012 by Dary Stone, outgoing regent and former chairman, to move me into an outside role. Dary guided the conversation—both over dinner at the Crescent and over breakfast at the Flying Fish (both in Dallas)—toward my finding professional happiness. "Judge, we want you to be happy." He was immensely charming and winsome.

The narrative that had emerged from Pat Neff Hall and Clifton Robinson Tower was to this effect: Judge's abiding passion was the law, and thus he would be more fulfilled in an outside role (such as chancellor) and the university would benefit from whatever fundraising and "friend-raising" skills I might bring to bear. Present for both those 2012 conversations, but largely silent throughout the Dary-Ken exchange, was the new chairman, Richard Willis. His turn came a year later—in the summer of 2013.

The setting was pleasant. After worship at Prestonwood Baptist in Plano, an extraordinarily vibrant megachurch, I joined Chairman Willis and Ron Murff, who chaired the powerful Governance Committee (known then as the Board and Administrative Affairs Committee), for Sunday dinner at the Bent Tree Country Club just north of the LBJ Freeway. The takeaway from our pleasant Sunday gathering was that in order to do a more comprehensive review of my performance as president, an outside consultant would be brought in to conduct a "360-degree" evaluation. I welcomed the idea.

Soon thereafter, I was contacted by Dr. Susan Resneck

Pierce, a former university president herself and a respected higher ed consultant. She did her work through telephone interviews from her office in Florida, submitting written questionnaires and the like. In October 2013, she came to campus for several days to complete her fact-finding.

Over breakfast at the Waco Hilton overlooking the Brazos, Susan opined that this was a highly unusual situation. I asked the what and how-so questions. She observed that the university, from all appearances, was doing very well, indeed prospering, that spirits were high and the faculty seemed at peace. Yet there was something awry. I was clueless, but effused about the university, the camaraderie around the Executive Council round table (even with the structural change from the year before), and the like. We bade farewell, but confirmed that we would meet several days later for a wrap-up session.

Susan completed her on-campus visits, and we reconvened once more over breakfast at the Hilton. Once again, she opined that this was one of the most unusual situations she'd ever encountered in higher ed. The university was doing well, but the board had made a decision. My contract, which had two years remaining (until June 1, 2015), would not be renewed.

I was thunderstruck. Yet again, I posed the how and why questions. A consummate professional, Susan made it clear that I wasn't what the board had in mind as CEO, but that I could usefully play a different role in university-wide leadership. I pressed for examples of my purported shortcomings. I protested that the board had—for three straight years—given me highly favorable, laudatory reviews, including just months before in the spring of 2013. I hadn't been guided or directed to any failing in my service.

I was genuinely perplexed. But my mind flashed back to the Crescent and the Flying Fish, and the departing Dary's gentle nudges to move me up and out. I was also keenly aware that Ken Hall, now the head of development (after his stellar career as CEO for the ministry of Buckner International) was openly telling folks on and off campus that I would be replaced as president—and he would be my replacement. From all that appears, Ken—and others in the administration—were seeking my ouster (or transfer to the chancellorship). In response, Susan flagged the fact that I hadn't attended meetings of the outside Investment Committee, which provided advice and guidance to our high-performing investment office headed by Dr. Brian Webb. That was it. No other examples.

My response was simple: I have nothing to add or contribute to the Investment Committee. That was simply not anywhere near my area of expertise. My time, I said with some fervor, was directed toward building Baylor, to connecting with the students, to encouraging the faculty, to restoring unity, to generating enthusiasm on the part of Baylor Nation, to raising money, to building stronger ties to the Waco community, and so on. Susan acknowledged that my three years and four months of service had been successful by all measures, but the board wanted me to take on a different role.

My quick calculation yielded up a very undesirable scenario. To have a new president in place on June 1, 2015, when my contract would expire, a search process would need to be launched within a matter of months—likely early 2014. At that point I would overnight become a lame duck. The university's initiatives, as I saw it, would be put on hold. I was perplexed.

Susan then added an intriguing footnote. She said that she asked the board whether she should be the one to deliver the news that my contract wouldn't be renewed. She was told yes. Susan was to be the messenger. My service was appreciated, but I should move into a new role with the board's enthusiastic encouragement and support.

My reaction was strong but restrained. "Susan, the bonds of trust have been dissolved. I can no longer serve. I'll resign." I put the point in context. I drew a story from my earlier service on the executive committee of my former law firm, Kirkland & Ellis. A nonequity partner had violated firm policy (but not any federal or state law) by investing in a client's enterprise without disclosing that investment to the firm. The question before the firm's executive committee was what to do. We considered various alternatives. As the conversation unfolded, a brilliant senior partner, Howard Krane, who at the time was chairing the Board of Trustees of the University of Chicago, offered his judgment: "By his actions, he has dissolved the bonds of trust. He should leave the firm." We all agreed. What Howard Krane had said years before, I told Susan, applied to my own unhappy situation.

Susan tried to be reassuring. The board didn't want me to go away, but just complete my remaining months of service and simply shift over to more of an outside role. I stood firm. I would resign as a matter of principle.

Within days, I was back with Richard Willis and Ron Murff. The setting was Floyd Casey Stadium, just before the West Virginia-Baylor football game. I told them face to face that the bonds of trust had been dissolved. I recounted my service in the Reagan Administration, when I'd been chief of staff to the attorney general. Although not close to

President Reagan, I'd watched him closely. I greatly admired his style of leadership. It was leadership based on first principles, then choosing the right people to implement and carry out those principles and goals.

I picked the example of national security. "President Reagan focused carefully on issues of foreign policy and national security. But if you asked, 'Mr. President, how many B-1 bombers are there in the fleet?' I'll bet he wouldn't know the precise answer. He would know the role of the B-1, but not their number. It's a different style of leadership."

The response came loud and clear: "We think the president should know the number of B-1 bombers in the fleet."

And so there it was—a conflict of visions about what the CEO was to be at Baylor University. For whatever reason, it was the first time this honest difference of opinion—or vision—had surfaced.

We left the meeting without any resolution or even agreement on next steps, and headed back to the game. I ran, perhaps a step or two quicker, with the Baylor Line (the freshmen, who by tradition run onto the field to welcome the team as they enter the stadium from the dressing room). As matters stood on that chilly October night, the bonds of trust had been dissolved. I left at halftime. Never before, or since, had I left my duty station in the president's suite. But we'd entered a radically different phase in the president-board relationship.

I don't know in any detail what happened in the board's discussions. But the upshot was that Richard Willis and Ron Murff soon came to me as if nothing had happened, armed with an attractive proposal. The board wanted me to remain as president. My contract would be extended for two years, until June 1, 2017. There was a helpful add-on—I would also assume the role of chancellor. I was pleased and relieved. The bonds of trust were being restored. I loved Baylor. I loved my job. I wanted to continue.

And so it was until the fall of 2015, when the Pepper Hamilton work began and negotiations resumed with the BAA. A great hero of mine, Judge Ed Kinkeade, reached out to Dean Brad Toben of Baylor Law School as well as to me. We commenced an intensive period of planning and negotiation with the BAA's leadership. Litigation, including terribly expensive and divisive pretrial discovery, was continuing apace as the university sought to end the longstanding agreements with the BAA. I soon stepped out of the process, which was then guided from the university's perspective by Richard Willis and Cary Gray, a board member and highly accomplished lawyer in Houston. Intense negotiations brought about the long-awaited "treaty" of peace. Unity was restored.

In early June 2016, the BAA—now reconstituted as the Baylor Line Foundation—held a celebratory dinner. The principal honoree, fittingly, was Judge Kinkeade, who I said over and over again deserved a Nobel Peace Prize for his singular role in getting the successful negotiations jump-started. The long-sought goal of unity had been accomplished.

In the meantime, I'd left the post of president of the university I'd come to love. And as a matter of conscience, I voluntarily stepped down as chancellor when terms to which I couldn't agree were put before me in a special meeting at Allbritton House, the president's home, on May 31. Like all good things, my service to Baylor had drawn to a close.

Scripture teaches that the generations come and the

generations go, but the earth remains forever. My own time had come and gone, but the longstanding desire of the regents leadership had been achieved. I would no longer serve as president of a great institution. But life marches on—and so does that good old Baylor Line.

11

REFLECTIONS

GETTING CASHIERED—ESPECIALLY SUDDENLY AS IF HIT BY LIGHTning—is no picnic or walk in the park. It's wrenching. It hurts. But it's also revealing. A spouse of one senior Baylor official, who years ago had been summarily sacked by the powers-that-be at the time, told Alice: "You find out who your friends are."

Amen. When you get your walking papers, some former colleagues who you counted as friends will avert their gaze or move to another part of the room. Or, as more frequently occurred, colleagues who for years had been in regular email correspondence abruptly check out without even saying "So sorry" or "Godspeed." But that's the way it is. As Judge Robert Bork was wont to say in reflecting on the latest manifestation of a fallen world, "Ah, well...." It was his simple way of observing: "The world is imperfect, but life goes on."

Happily, that understandable (if less than admirable) response of "I don't know you anymore" is truly the exception, at least within the Baylor family. Baylor Bears are, by overwhelming numbers, kind and gracious folks who care about one another. They don't like to see anyone hurt. And the outpouring of love and affection to both Alice and me has been little short of overwhelming. It began with students coming to Allbritton House, unannounced, and expressing their empathy and support. These unexpected visits were a balm to the soul and a lift to sagging spirits. At times, one had a sense that a faculty member or administrator was visiting clandestinely, like Nicodemus of old, not necessarily eager to be seen.

My sudden firing as president, and subsequent resignation from the chancellorship as a matter of conscience, also sparked a much-needed set of reflections on my part with respect to American culture, particularly the subculture of free-flowing alcohol and casual sex on (or, more precisely, around) college campuses. Sadly, but unsurprisingly, Baylor has not been insulated from the winds of enormous social change, including the execrable hook-up culture that infects so much of contemporary life. No lesser light than Tom Wolfe captured the baleful manifestation of runaway promiscuity on American campuses in his troubling novel *I Am Charlotte Simmons.* Making bad matters worse, policy makers in Washington, D.C. have decided that the fundamental problem lies with institutions, not with individuals in their own personal conduct.

At the center of the present-day cultural finger-pointing is the Department of Education, and in particular its Office of Civil Rights. Responding to deeply troubling reports of all-too-frequent incidents of sexual violence (the term employed by the federal enforcement authorities is "interpersonal violence"), OCR issued a highly controversial "Dear Colleague" letter in April 2011 setting forth guidance for colleges and universities with respect to preventing and responding to acts of interpersonal violence.

The fount of this assertion of sweeping federal authority is Title IX of the Education Amendments of 1972. Everyone can understand what the statute says; no need to go to law school (or even recall a basic civics course in high school) to comprehend what Congress was doing back during the tempestuous days of the Nixon Administration. The words of Title IX are admirably succinct, yet capaciously inclusive: "No person in the United States shall, on the basis of sex, be excluded from participation in, be denied the benefits of, or be subjected to discrimination under any education program or activity receiving Federal financial assistance." That's the entire law; one sentence, completely straightforward in its meaning. The key element in triggering this important requirement is the receipt of "federal financial assistance," which includes of course virtually every higher ed institution.

For an entire generation, Title IX did laudable, widely heralded work. Especially for an intentional culture-shifting statute, the measure was blissfully uncontroversial yet highly productive. As with Title VII of the 1964 Civil Rights Act (prohibiting racial and similar forms of discrimination in employment), Title IX was a genuine reform measure heralding a new day in American law and culture. That new reality had very high visibility, especially with respect to women's athletics on college campuses. This was grist for the mill of a new phenomenon, namely all-sports television. With ever-greater sports programming content, including women's sports, ESPN was launched in 1979, an intriguing coincidence in light of the timing of the door-opening effects of Title IX.

This societal commitment to inclusiveness and equity ushered in important new opportunities for women. Additional sports (such as equestrian and acrobatics-tumbling) were embraced by previously male-dominated college athletic programs. Baylor specifically has been blessed by those two new sports, which attracted wonderful, talented students literally from across the country. In short, Title IX's strictures moved intercollegiate sports generally— and Baylor specifically—to a much better, fairer place. And across the country, not just on ESPN, Americans can see the abundant fruits of Title IX's labors year in and year out, especially at the Olympics, where American women now dominate in many sports.

These days, however, the prototypical Title IX "event" isn't the launching of a new women's sports program or a fairer, more open workplace but a report of a tragedy filled with profound sorrow and deep anger. It is, in short, an act of interpersonal violence—student on student. This nightmare scenario typically occurs off campus at an event that's neither sponsored nor sanctioned by the university. Indeed, consistent with traditional Christian teaching, Baylor has a clear policy proscribing sex outside of marriage. So too, alcohol is prohibited on campus. Go to a Baylor campus event and the strongest beverages available are iced tea and Dr Pepper. And it won't do to sneak in a flask; sanctions for noncompliance can be significant.

Notwithstanding these clear policies, which secularists derisively dismiss as hopelessly out of fashion, OCR holds Baylor—and other universities—accountable for what happens totally off campus, after hours (typically, late-night parties) and without the slightest indicia of Baylor sponsorship. Indeed, in light of Baylor's policies, these off-campus venues are today's equivalent of a Chicago speakeasy coupled with alcohol-sotted sexual adventures. But whether a mocking, scoffing media will agree or not, Baylor is entirely within its lawful prerogatives in America's constitutional framework to define its policies and establish its institutional values. The baseline is freedom to say who we are and what we stand for.

Not only Christian institutions, but every single college and university in America is wrestling with the following question: Under Title IX's language, does an off-campus event or episode—involving tragedy and possibly crime—really and truly trigger institutional responsibility under federal law when the college had absolutely zero to do with planning or hosting the event?

By its terms, the statute doesn't readily lend itself to a positive answer to that question. In the typical example of the new Title IX world faced by college administrators, where—in the language of Title IX—is the "program" or "activity" of the university? The key language, as passed by Congress and signed into law by President Nixon, doesn't seem to apply.

To be sure, if the university does in fact sponsor an event or activity, or perhaps even if a university-recognized group sponsors an event or activity, the jurisdictional trigger becomes clear—or at least arguably does. But the current framework for Title IX, as erected over time by OCR, has led colleges and universities to assume practical responsibility for both prevention of interpersonal violence off campus and effective and fair responsiveness with respect to any such alleged acts.

There's a remarkable irony here, however. The much-ballyhooed April 2011 "Dear Colleague" letter from OCR nowhere suggests an automatic responsibility by the institution for what happens off campus. Rather, the letter by its terms suggests a much more limited sweep. Only if the off-campus event or episode has an on-campus effect, namely the creation of a "hostile environment" on campus, is Title IX implicated. How would that happen—a terrible event off campus somehow affecting campus life and culture? OCR provides the example: "If a student alleges that he or she was sexually assaulted by another student off school grounds, and that upon returning to school he or she was taunted or harassed by other students who are the alleged perpetrator's friends, the school should take the earlier school assault into account in determining whether there is a sexually hostile environment."

Note this vitally important limitation: The "Dear Colleague" letter isn't focusing on whether an act of interpersonal violence occurred. That's the backdrop or context, but it's not the Title IX triggering event. The key is whether, in the wake of an alleged sexual assault, a hostile environment is created on campus. That is, the core question for college administrators—and trustees and regents—is whether there's exclusion or denial of participation in campus life, not whether there was an off-campus incident.

In my experience and observation, that inquiry is no longer the focus on the now-elaborate Title IX adjudicatory process. To the contrary, as industry practice (so to speak) has developed, literally the only question being resolved is whether an act of interpersonal violence was committed, regardless of the location or venue. If so, as determined by the standard of "preponderance of the evidence," then the student who is charged with sexual assault (the "respondent") will be held liable (deemed "responsible"), with sanctions that can be and frequently are quite severe.

The stakes, in short, are exceptionally high—on both sides, as well as for the institution. A shattering, dignity-denying experience on the part of the victim (the "complainant"), with potentially grave emotional and psychological harm; a stress-filled on-campus adjudicatory procedure for both parties; and a process that may eventuate in the termination of a student's educational journey (or at least its significant disruption).

What's to be done? To be sure, as a moral imperative, colleges and universities should have a robust training, prevention, and responsive process. It's the right thing to do. We care deeply about our students and their welfare. In particular, greater emphasis is being placed on bystander awareness and intervention. If something bad is about to happen, friends should step in, intervene, and get the potential victim out of harm's way.

But it's also time for a reassessment of where we are in American higher education. There's a limit to what any institution can do with respect to emancipated young adults who aren't participating in a university event or activity when a horrific event occurs. Yes, "It's on Us" prevention campaigns are important. But at the heart of the problem is the ancient one—decisions by individuals on what to do with their own lives.

At Baylor, the culture must be one of encouragement to do the right thing, and the deepening of a caring community, but not the creation of a police state. When the concerned parent understandably asks, "What assurance do you have that my student won't be the subject of interpersonal violence or sexual assault?" the appropriate response is: "We're all in this together. We'll do our best to do our part. Your student likewise has a responsibility." More bluntly, but in truth, the caring administrator can say: "Guide your student not to go to late-night off-campus parties. And if, even in the face of your loving guidance, your student does go, he or she should be on guard—and not let down that guard by failing to engage in self-control and self-discipline."

Kevin Jackson, as head of Baylor's Division of Student Life, uses the very apt analogy of "Friends don't let friends drive" when the would-be driver is obviously impaired for whatever reason. Wise students avoid the spider's web of alcohol-abusing behavior and the wee-hours gatherings that give rise to that abuse.

And wise parents, loved ones, trustees, and regents will come alongside the always-challenged administrators and find ways to be supportive and encouraging—and thereby foster the flourishing of the caring community that colleges—especially Christian universities—are, at their very best.

That is certainly, at its best, the Baylor Way. While administrators, including university presidents, come and go, this truth abides through thick and thin—Baylor will continue, by God's grace, to be "for the church" and "for Texas," a vibrant and caring community that serves as a warm and welcoming lighthouse for a hurting world.

12

COMMENCEMENT

THE OLD NOSTRUM, "WHEN IT RAINS, IT POURS," PROVED PAINFULLY apposite during the long summer and autumn of 2016. News reports continued to cascade with respect to Title IX, Pepper Hamilton, and the institutional and personal nightmare that began on August 20, 2015 with the *Texas Monthly* online report about the Sam Ukwuachu trial. The extended Baylor family was long since ready to close the tragic chapter and turn the page. Yet, the story stubbornly plunged ahead, spilling over into the new academic year (2016–2017). Then, in October 2016 came the startling, headline-grabbing resignation of Patty Crawford, Baylor's deeply pastoral, caring, and full-time coordinator of Title IX. Her announcement was trumpeted nationally, led by her *CBS Morning News* in-studio interview.

In short order, reports emerged that *60 Minutes* (CBS) and the *Wall Street Journal* were poking around. ESPN, which had mischaracterized information that came to Coach Briles about Sam Ukwuachu's departure at Boise State, continued its drumbeat.

How to think about all this unflattering and at times scathingly biting attention sharply focused on a great university with its storied history?

In an interview with *Texas Tribune* cofounder Evan Smith in late September 2016, I drew a sharp distinction

between the metanarrative created in media portraits on
the one hand, and what I simply called "reality." Reality is
that good people and great institutions are consigned to
live in a fallen world, and bad things—at times very bad
things—will occur.

In the face of tragedy and disaster, the unifying
Christian principles of redemption and grace provide
warm and welcome assurance that the storms of life will
eventually subside, so long as by God's good grace the
steely determination exists to try to do better. History—
and abiding theological truths—become sources of succor,
an eagerly welcome "balm in Gilead." That heavenly
reassurance— "Oh, what a foretaste of glory divine"—calms
the soul and lifts the spirit. As the deeply moving song of
the church teaches, "When sorrows like sea billows roll,
whatever my lot, Thou has taught me to say, It is well, it is
well with my soul."

Soul. In a figurative sense, an institution likewise has
a soul, a spirit that endures after the present generation
has taken its bow, the curtain has fallen, and a new cast of
dramatis personae takes its place on stage. But my favorite
metaphor for Baylor—and for Christian higher education
more generally—is the lighthouse. To seafaring folk, the
seas are beautiful but dangerous, forbidding places; the
lights of shore are comforting symbols of hearth and home,
of safe harbors from wind and wave. The lighthouse bids
the intrepid sailors farewell as their departing ship sails
from port, and then at voyage's end welcomes them home
again. Even after their practical need has disappeared in the
wake (so to speak) of technological progress, lighthouses
remain. They stand as towering reminders of the dangers
of life, yet more comfortingly the fierce determination at

the heart of the human spirit not only to survive, but to carry on, to press forward, and to flourish.

That's the Baylor spirit. Its symbol could well be the lighthouse, rather than the beloved bear with its fierce independence. In its way, the statue of Judge Baylor and the spires of Pat Neff Hall do splendid service as the Baylor lighthouse. How reassuring that, in the face of maddeningly unfavorable publicity and the wrenching institutional decisions of May 2016 culminating in my own firing and ensuing resignation, Baylor has flourished. This great university bearing Judge Baylor's good name is no phoenix-like figure rising from the ashes. Quite the contrary. This is Baylor. This is the determined, steady march of the Baylor Line, with its indomitable spirit and fierce commitment to carry on in the face of adversity.

How comforting it was in mid-August 2016 to witness the incoming class of 2020 coming to campus and taking its place, with impressive statistics of success and qualifications that embodied a story of continuing progress and a grace-filled future. Capturing the continuing determination that Baylor would press forward in the face of sorrows, tragedies, and vicious media onslaughts was the fact that yet again Baylor was self-anointed by faculty and staff as a great college to work for.

May that always be. And by God's grace, it will be. Baylor University and the magical Baylor Line, joining in hearty chorus to sing together the great celebratory song of unity: "We march forever down the years, as long as stars shall shine." We march *pro ecclesia* (for the church); *pro Texana* (for Texas and the world); and *pro futuris* (for the future).